MINDS

by

Dave Sim and Gerhard

Aardvark-Vanaheim Inc.
First printing: (limited signed and numbered) June 1996
Second printing: June 1996
Third printing: June 1998
Fourth Printing: August 2001

ISBN 0-919359-16-7

Printed in Windsor, Ontario by
Preney Print & Litho Inc.

PRINTED IN CANADA

Introduction:

It's very difficult to write an introduction to this, the fourth book of *Mothers and Daughters*, without giving away too much of the actual story. I had a specific intention for this fourth book, way, way back, when I was still working on *Church and State*. For the longest time, the final third of this very book was the furthest outpost in the Cerebus journey that I had marked clearly on my mental Cerebus map. It ties together many, if not most, of the loose ends which have been left dangling through Our Story Thus Far. It is difficult to write this introduction because I don't want to "give away" the crucial story point. So, let me just say that my conception of the story was carved in stone some time ago and that much of the writing — the tying-off-loose-ends part — was largely a challenge of distillation. And what a relief and a terror it was — putting down on the page the sequence of events and repercussions from way, way, *way* back in 1977, '78, and '79, answering the *who*, *what*, *where*, *when*, and *why*'s I've been keeping secret for nearly twenty years.

It's not easy keeping a secret for twenty years, you know.

And then, having discharged my obligations in the area of tying off loose ends, I came at last to the point I thought I would *never* get to.

"Your turn."

And after that simple two-word dialogue balloon, it was time for complete improvisation. As difficult as it is to keep a secret for twenty years, it is at least (*at least*) as difficult to keep a secret from yourself for that long. I had no idea what Cerebus's dialogue would be from that point on. For close to ten years, I wouldn't let myself even *speculate* on it as I lived with the little gray bastard (hey, he's mine — I can say that) day in and day out. I had to trust that such an extended period of living with the title character of this large and strange experiment would make the improvisation go well, but I had no way of knowing. Disconcerting indeed, when the capstone to a 1,000-page sequence, and (in many ways) the capstone to the entire previous 4,000 pages, hinges on such a nebulous article of faith. Keeps me interested anyway.

I hope the exhilaration of the roller-coaster ride from "Your turn" to the end of this particular book communicates half of the genuine enjoyment I experienced putting it down on paper in words and pictures. Hell, even a quarter of the enjoyment means you'll be getting your money's worth (I reckon).

When you're done, I hope you'll agree.

Now, if you'll recall the end of *Reads*, Cerebus and Cirin had just hurtled past the Moon on a chunk of rock which also holds the Papal Throne from the now-demolished Eastern Church of Tarim. As we rejoin the unlikely duo . . .

Dave Sim
Kitchener, Ontario
May 1, 1996

book four
minds

13

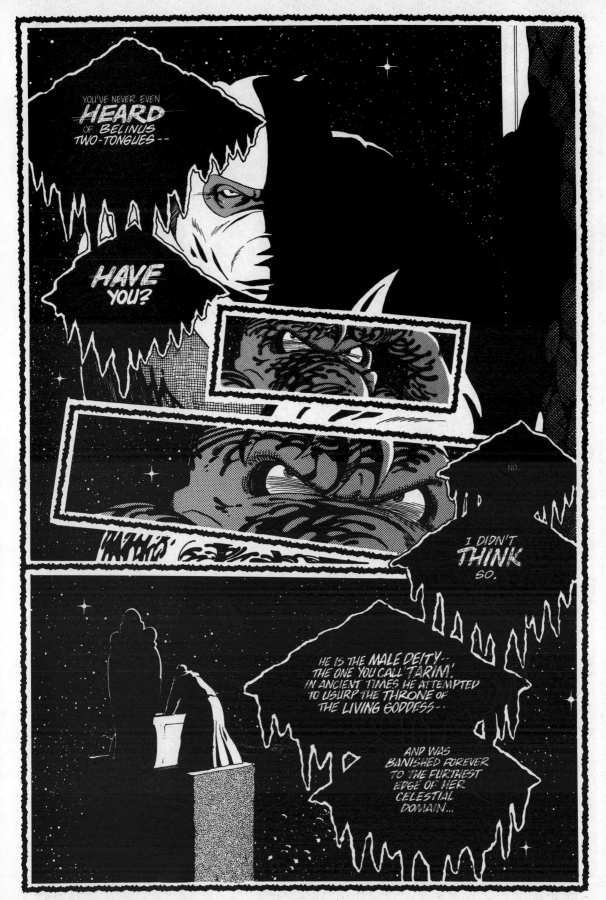

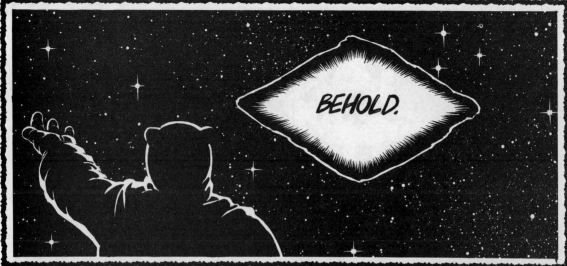

BEHOLD.

"BEHOLD: HER FIRMAMENT.
BEHOLD: HER PROGENY
WITHOUT NUMBER.
BEHOLD: THE MILK OF
HER BOSOM ARCHING
FROM INFINITY TO
INFINITY."

YOU CAN'T BE *SERIOUS*. CLOVIS IS A CONSTRUCT OF TARIMITE MISSIONARIES -- A MERGING OF THE BOREALAN THUNDER-GOD, *BAAN*, AND THE TARIMITE STAR-SON MYTHOLOGY...

OH, *YEAH?* WELL, WHY DON'T YOU *TELL* HIM THAT WHILE HE'S *WINDING YOUR ENTRAILS AROUND THE WHEELS OF HIS WAR CHARIOT?!*

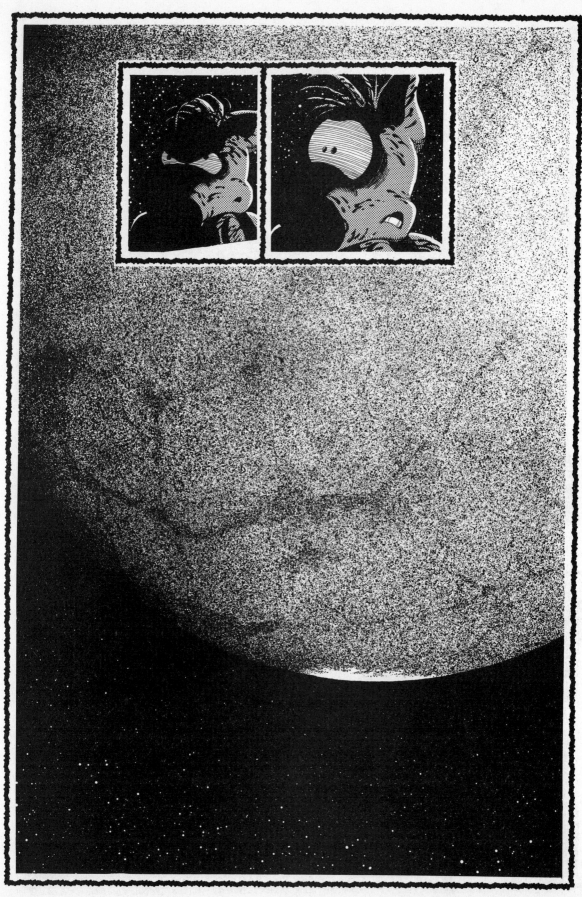

THE SPHERE OF PURIFICATION.

OF CLEANSING.

OF ...HEALING.

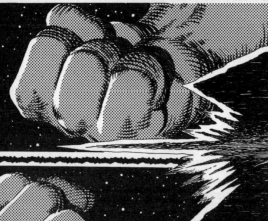

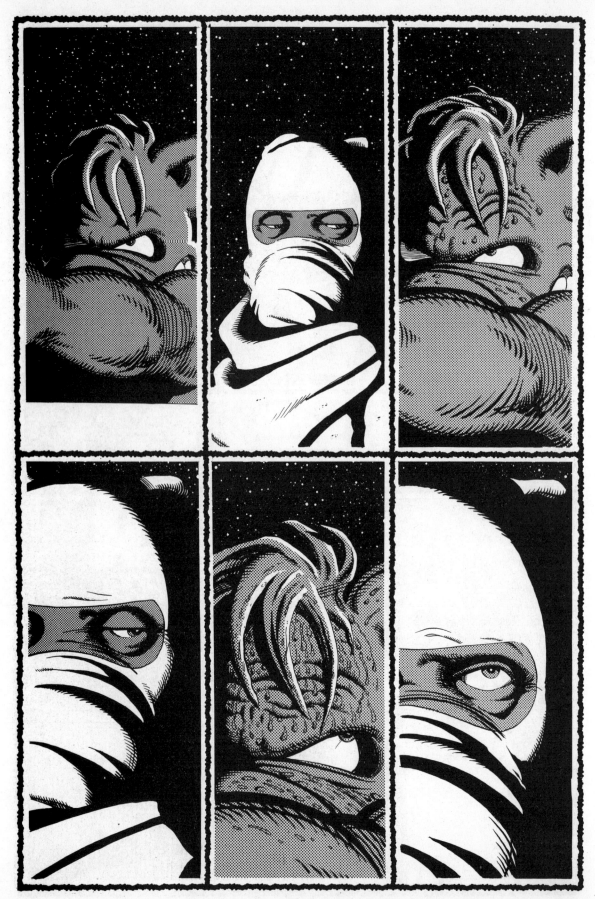

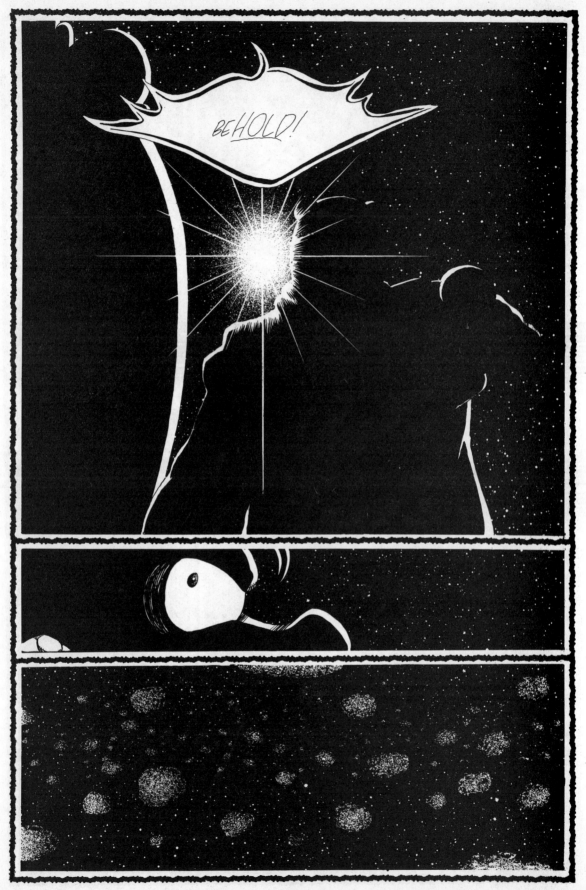

FINAL RESTING PLACE FOR THOSE WHOSE HEARTS HAD TURNED FROM THE LOVE OF OUR LADY...

WORSHIPPERS OF MALE DEITIES, FORNICATORS, REBELLIOUS DAUGHTERS, MYSTICS, PRACTITIONERS OF CONTRACEPTION...

RAPISTS, MURDERERS,

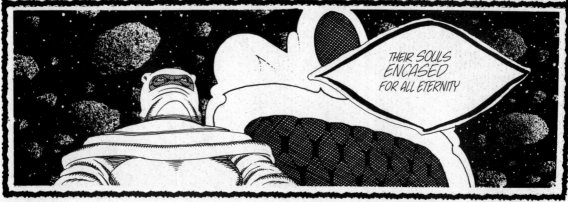

THEIR SOULS ENCASED FOR ALL ETERNITY

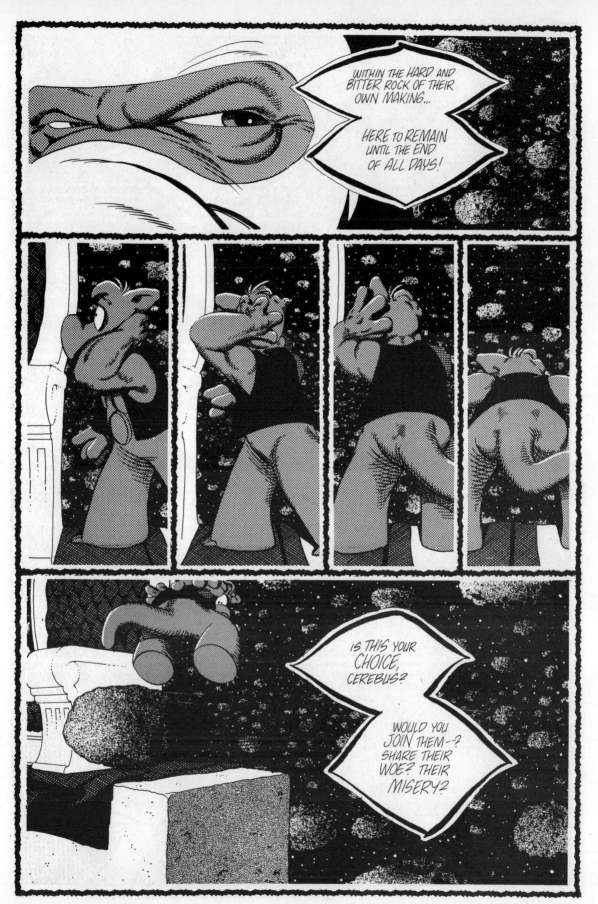

35

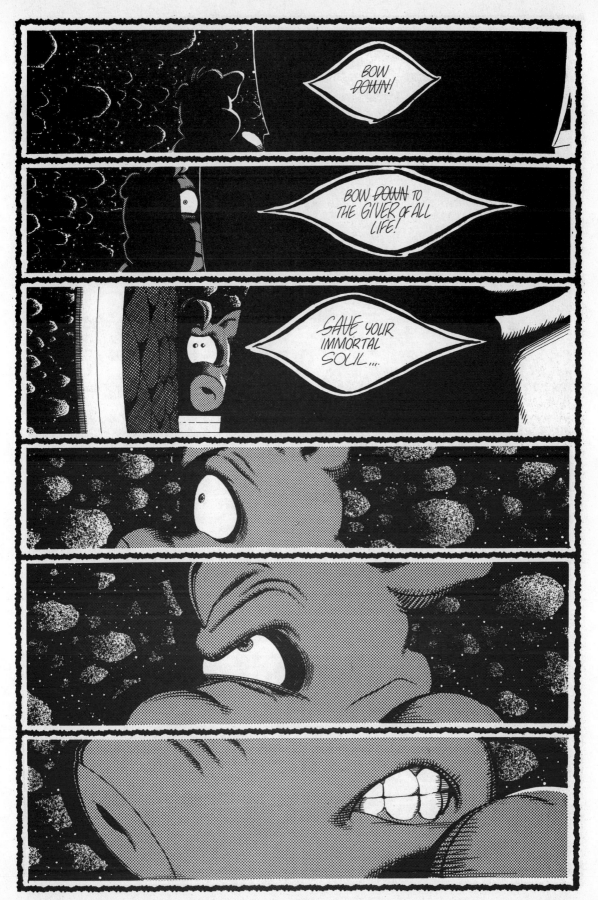

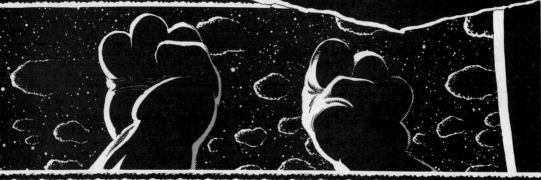

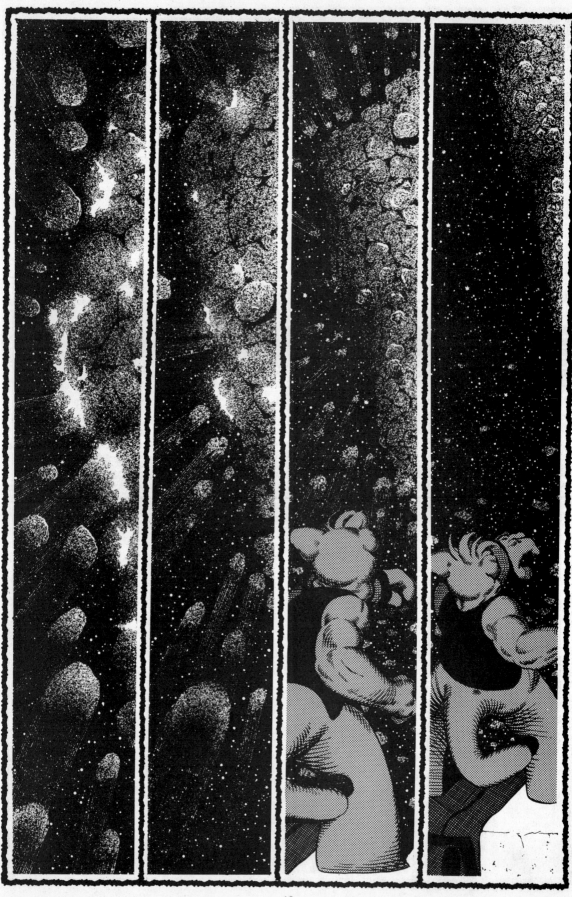

43

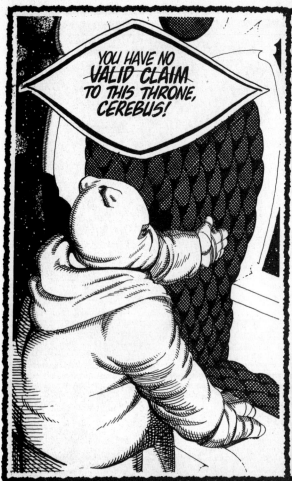

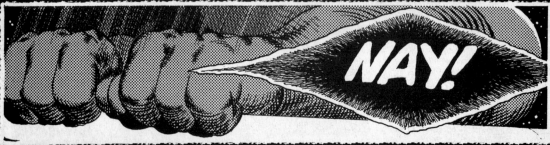

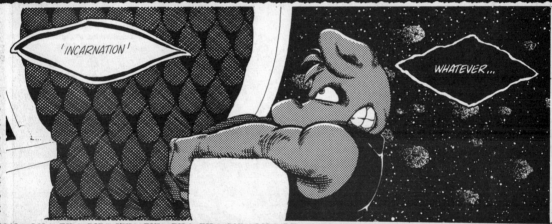

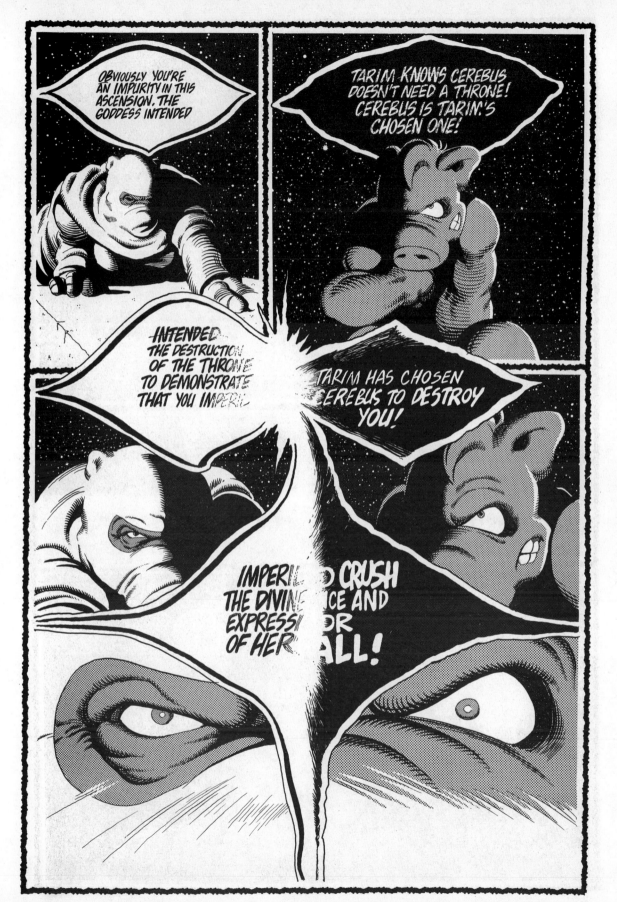

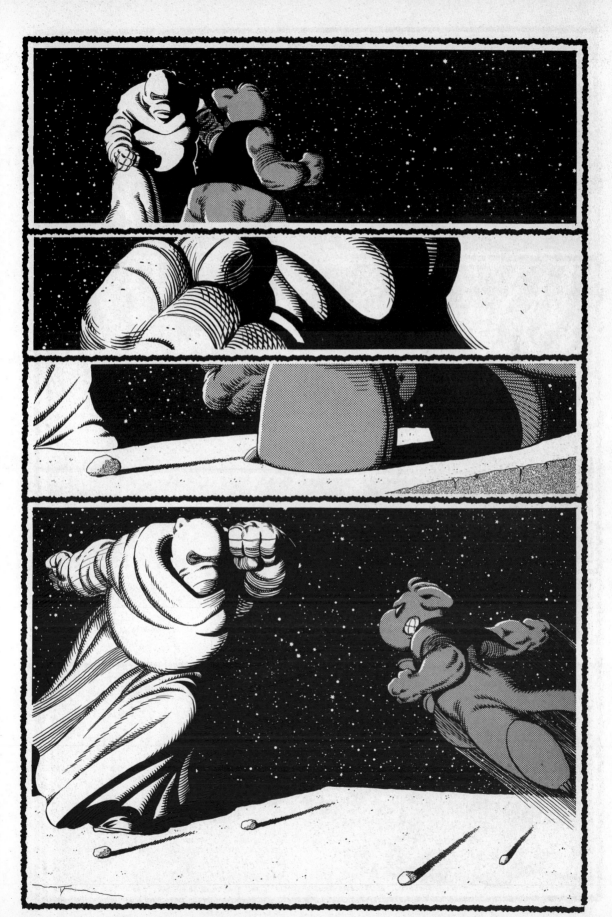

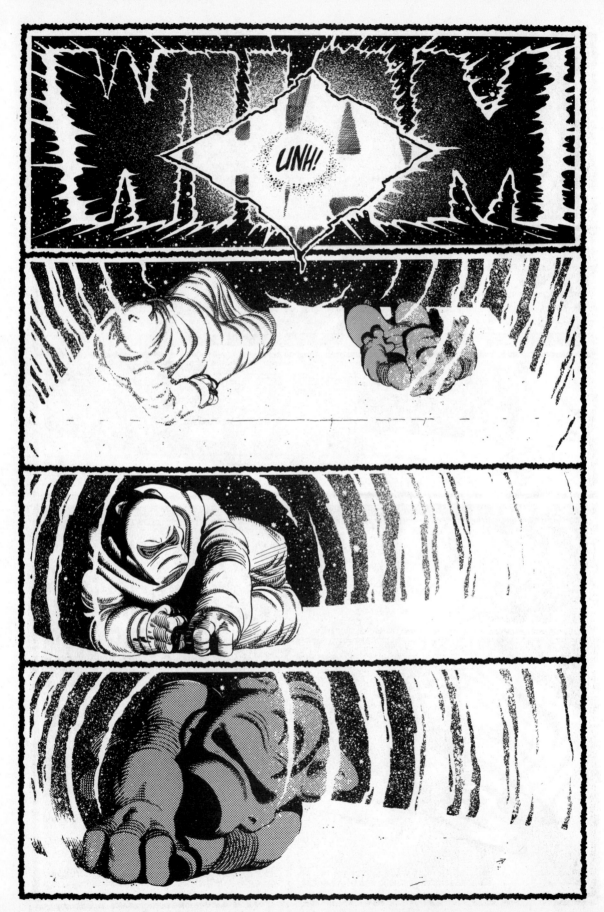

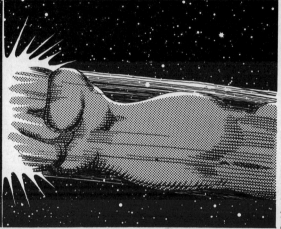

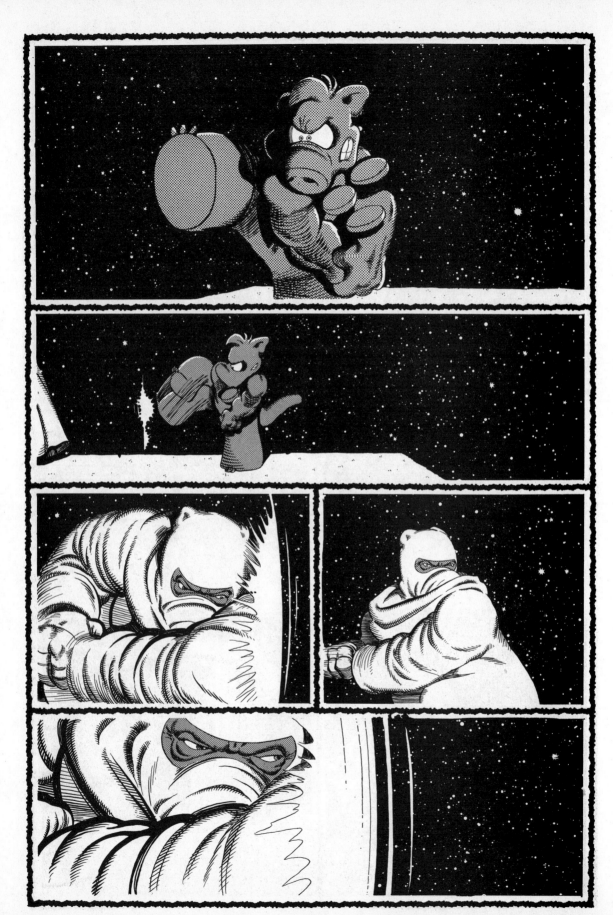

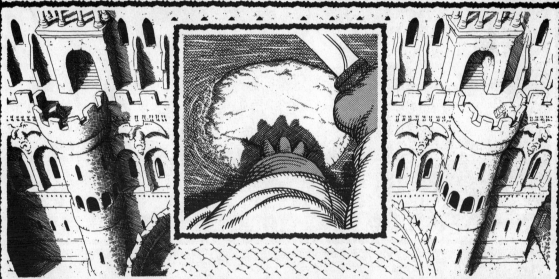

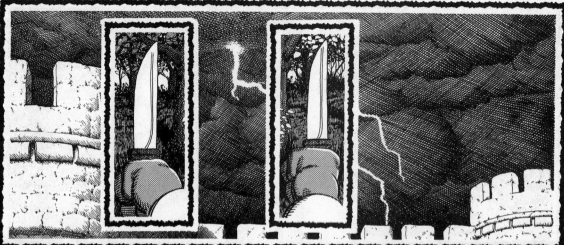

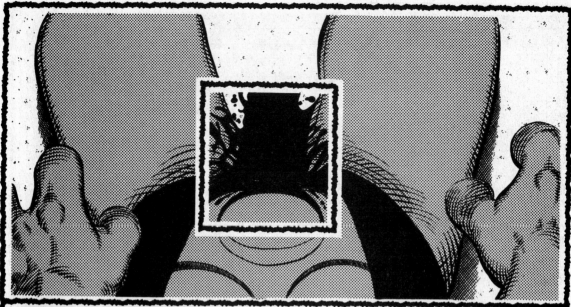

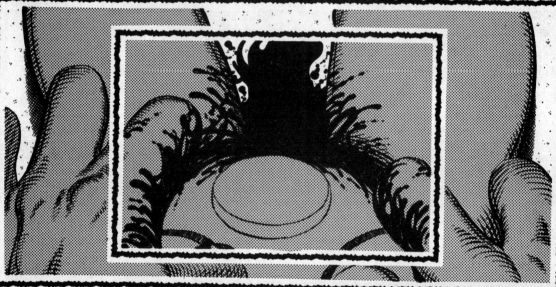

Vicar Graeme _is_ a drunkard and an adulterer.

WELL, YEAH-- O'COURSE. EVERYBODY KNOWS THAT.

BUT Y'DON'T GO SHOUTING IT ALL OVER THE _MARKET SQUARE_

≈sigh≈ Why have you brought your son to me, carpenter?

WELL. YOU'RE A _MAGICIAN_-- I THOUGHT-- YOU KNOW...

YOU'D HAVE A POTION OR A... _SPELL_ OR SOMETHING.

SETTLE 'IM DOWN A BIT. SO 'E'S LIKE THE OTHER BOYS.

I see.

And what if your son is _correct_? What if he _IS_ the chosen one?

AYE?

WOT?

_MY_ CEREBUS? THE ...THE ... _WELL!_

I MEAN WHAT ARE THE ODDS O' _THAT?_

The Will of Tarim is not a dog race, carpenter.

To tamper with it To Miscalculate on the basis of... _Likelihood_...

... would be to invite Incalculable Consequence.

81

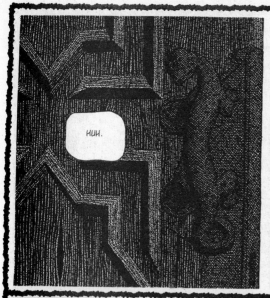

HUH.

What do you... *See* ... when you look at your son, carpenter?
...

OH-- uh .... THAT'S WHY WE GOT 'IM TH' *HAT.* 'IS MUM'S IDEA IT WAS.

KIDS CAN BE *CRUEL* CAN 'THEY? 'IS GREAT GRANDAD HAD BIG EARS, THAT'S WHERE 'E GOT 'EM FROM I EXPECT...

'IS GREAT GRANDAD

big ears.

and that's *all* that you see?

AYE.

WELL, I'M NO OIL PAIN'IN' MYSELF AM I? ... E'S SMALL FOR 'IS AGE, BUT SO WAS I ...

'E'LL SHOOT UP LIKE A *WEED* ONE O' THESE DAYS...

SEE IF HE DON'T

HE'S MY *BOY,* SEE? BEGGIN' Y' PARDON, BUT I DINT COME 'ERE T' DISCUSS 'IS *LOOKS*

IF Y'CAN HELP TO... SETTLE 'IM DOWN, I'LL BE HAPPY T'MEET YOUR PRICE. IF *NOT,* JUST *TELL ME*... AND WE'LL BE ON OUR WAY.

Whatever Is Within Your Son, Carpenter, Can No More Be 'Settled Down' By Means Of Elixir or Incantation Than Could The Sofim River.

However, Like A River, It Can Be Channeled.

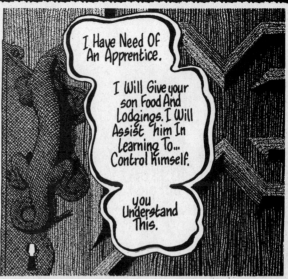

I Have Need Of An Apprentice.

I Will Give Your Son Food And Lodgings. I Will Assist Him In Learning To... Control Himself.

You Understand This.

AYE.

And You Will Reassure Your Good Wife That Cerebus Is Well-Cared-For.

WELL CARED-FOR.

The Two of You Will Enjoy This Small Jar Of Honey As You Discuss His New And Wonderful Opportunity.

NEW AND WONDERFUL OPPORTUNITY.

You Will, Of Course, Visit The Boy Any Time You Wish...

Between Sunrise And Noon.

VERY KIND OF YOU, SIR.

You Must Be Getting Home Now.

THANK YOU, SIR, BUT I MUST BE GETTING HOME NOW.

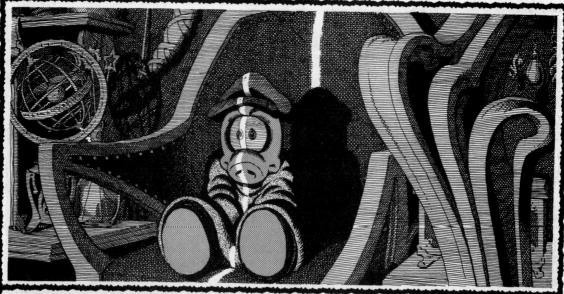

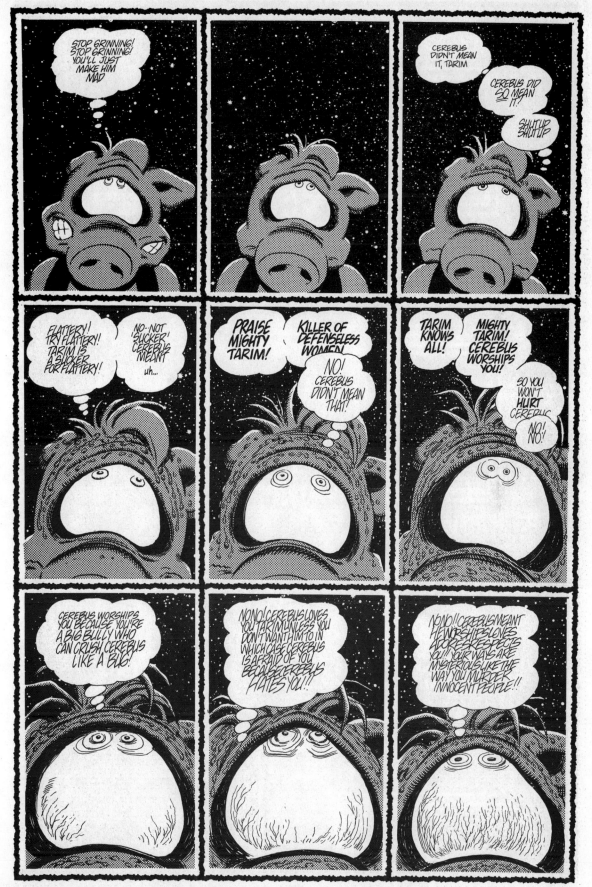

Whose Single CRIMSON EYE Sees into Ev'ry SOUL

so VAST that ALL the OCEANS in ALL the WORLD

are! to HIM! no more than the smallest part of the smallest drop of rain

AND WHEN YOUR DAY of JUDGEMENT COMES

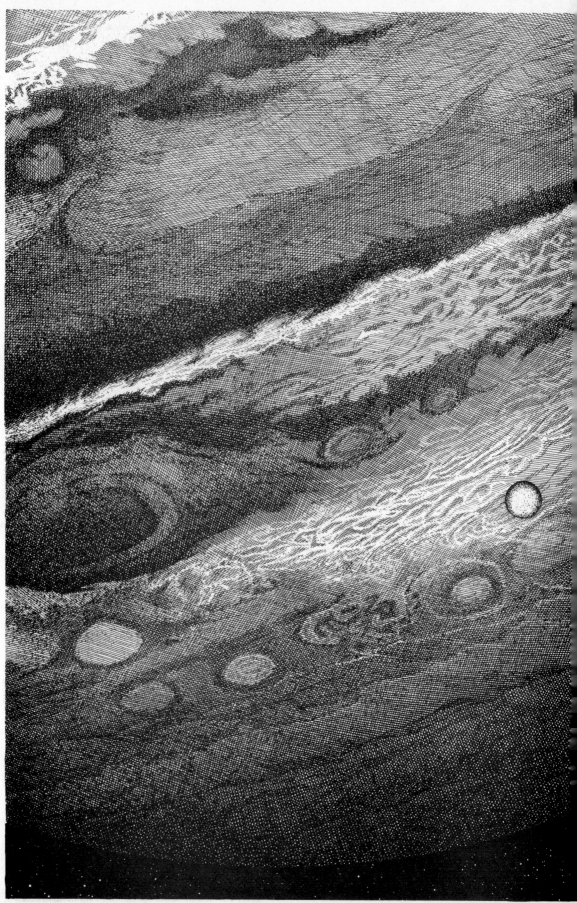

WILL YOU STAND BEFORE the LIVING TARIM AS ONE WHO KEPT HIS LAWS and REVERED HIS NAME? WILL YOU BE REWARDED by an ETERNITY of JOY? and PEACE?

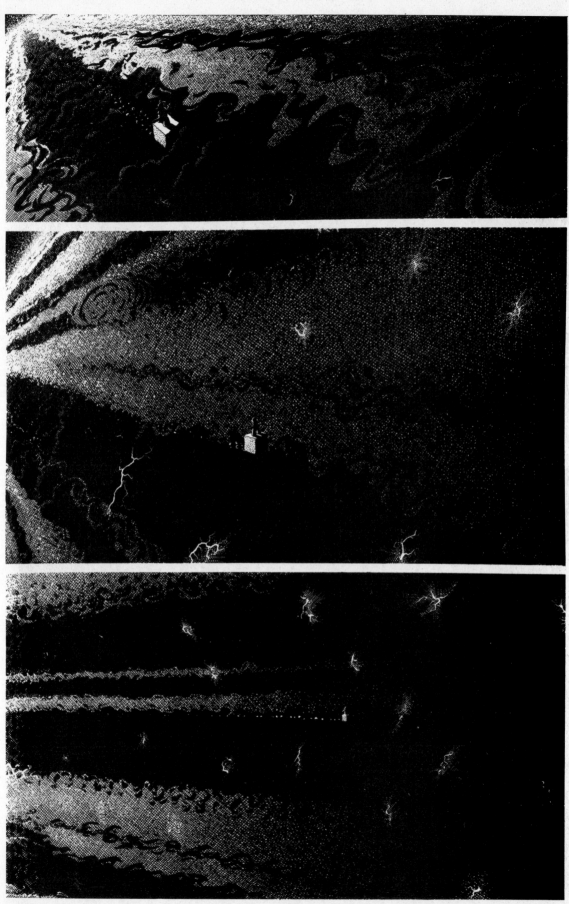

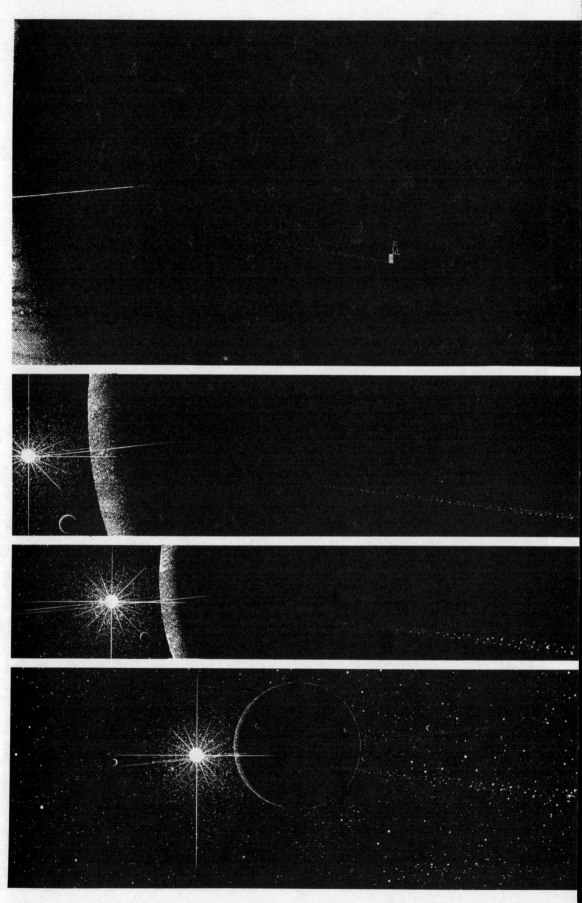

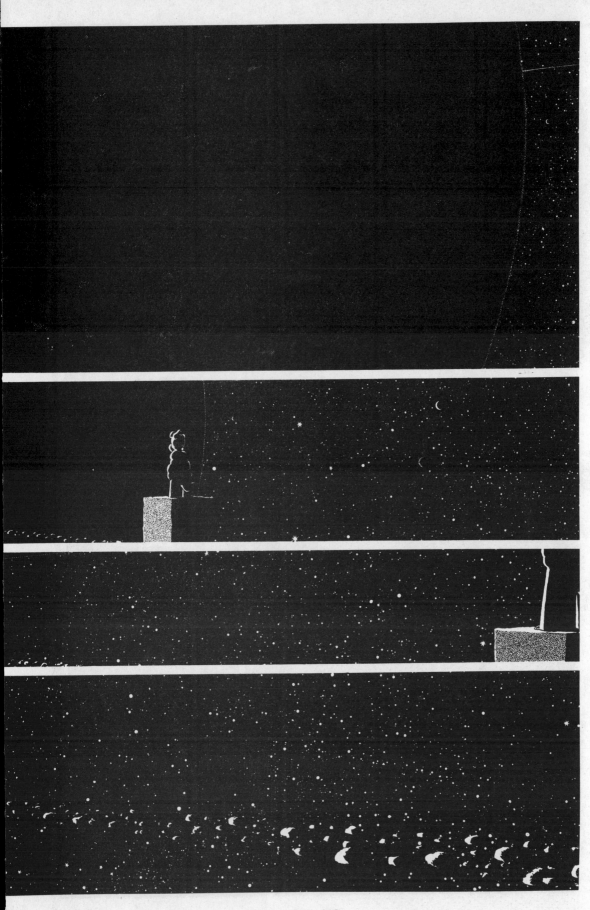

115

THAT'S A KIND OF *TRIBUTE.*

RIGHT?

'TARIM!'

'TARIM TARIM TARIM TARIM TARIM TARIM TARIM TARIM'

(AS IN)

'TARIM! THIS FOOD IS *GOOD!'*

'TARIM! CEREBUS GOT *REALLY DRUNK* LAST NIGHT!'

'TARIM! CEREBUS SURE WOULD LIKE TO BUGGER A ...'

WHAT CEREBUS IS TRYING TO *SAY* IS...

123

126

129

'STORIA DOESN' LOVE CER'BUS... NObUDDY LOVES CER'BUS.... PRIMINN ISSER DOESN' HAVENNY POWER

CER'BUSSES STILL BROKE'N ALL CERBUS WAN'SISS REAL POWER

NObUDDY DOES WHUD CERBUS TELLZEMADOO NObUDDY!! NObUDDY..... CERBUS JUSSWANNS PEOPLEA DO WHUDTHERR TOLD!!

'N' GOLD!! CERBUSWANSSA LODDAGOLD! AMOWNNinna GOLD---'N' CERBUSWANSSABE LEF'ALONE!

'FONLY ONE PERSON'D LOVE CER'BUS...

EVYbUDDY LIEza CERBUS....CERBUS DUZZEN' CARE IF THEY HADE CER'BUS... JUZbE HONEST...JUZ 'JUZ SAY: 'CER'BUS? I HADE YORE GUDDS!!'

CER'BUS JUZ WAN'SPEOPLE CERBUS C'N COUNT ON....

NODALLA 'ESE BACK STABBIN' TWO-FACED NO GOOD DOUBLE DEALIN' ≈HIC≈ ROCRUTS

SO ON,

AND uh

SOPHIA LOVED YOU... SHE KNEW YOU NEEDED TO FEEL LOVED, YOU WANTED LOTS OF SEX AND MOST OF THE TIME YOU WANTED TO BE LEFT ALONE

SO SHE DID ALL THREE AS BEST SHE COULD

AND HER MOTHER, OF COURSE, HATED YOUR GUTS AND WAS AS HONEST AS SHE COULD BE ON THE SUBJECT...

SHE THOUGHT:

HOW DO I EVEN *BEGIN* TO EXPLAIN TO HIM THAT I HAVE NO *ROMANTIC FEELINGS* FOR HIM AND THAT I HAVEN'T SINCE THE *GREENHOUSE?* THAT LOOK IN HIS EYES THAT I KNOW SO WELL. *MONEY*-HUNGRY. *POWER*-HUNGRY. NOT A DROP OF LOVE OR EVEN *SWEETNESS* LEFT FROM WHEN WE MET. IT'S AS IF I'M A PIECE OF JEWELRY HE MISPLACED OR SOMETHING -- AND HE'S COME TO RECLAIM IT AS THE RIGHTFUL OWNER. HOW VERY, VERY SAD. I'LL MAKE MEN JEALOUS OF HIM, HE'S THINKING, AND THAT JEALOUSY WILL FEED HIS HUNGER FOR POWER. YOU DON'T ASK A MISPLACED PIECE OF JEWELRY HOW IT *FEELS* OR WHAT IT *WANTS.* I'D ALMOST BE *ANGRY* -- ANGRY THAT HE'S SO BLIND TO MY LOVE OF RICK, MY HOME... DANCING -- IF IT DIDN'T MAKE ME FEEL SO SORRY FOR HIM. I CAN'T SHOW ANY SIGN OF ANGER OR PITY OR HE'S GOING TO LEAVE. AND *IF* HE LEAVES I HAVE A *STRONG FEELING* THAT SOMETHING *AWFUL* WILL HAPPEN TO HIM. *I'M SURE OF IT!* I HAVE TO SAY SOME- THING -- SOMETHING THAT WILL MAKE HIM STAY. *THINK, JAKA* -- *THINK!*

I'LL TELL HIM I'M AFRAID. I *HATE* TO LIE TO HIM, BUT I'LL TELL HIM I'M AFRAID. IT WILL MAKE HIM FEEL LIKE A -- A -- BODYGUARD OR SOMETHING. *'I'M NOT AFRAID OF YOU, BUT IT'S BECAUSE OF YOU THAT I'M AFRAID.'* IT MAKES NO SENSE, BUT COUPLED WITH THE PROTECTIVENESS HE FEELS TOWARD ME AND HIS VANITY IT MIGHT JUST BE ENOUGH TO MAKE HIM STAY -- AT *LEAST* UNTIL THESE AWFUL PREMONITIONS PASS

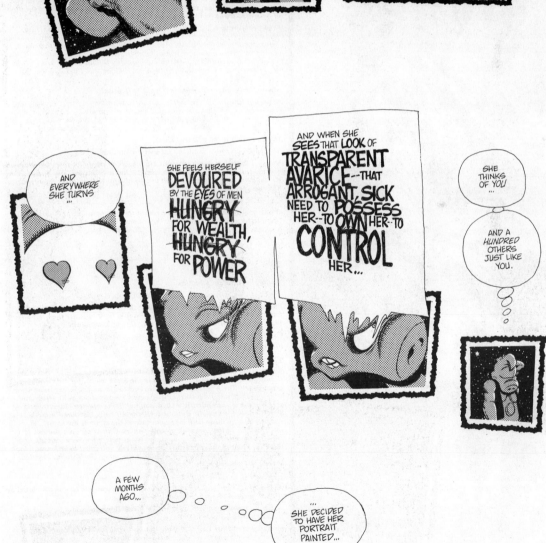

You see before you, gentle lady, the fruits of my labours as Chairman of the Palnan Arts Council. Every well-regarded painter in the land displayed in descending order of popularity. Of these none is more universally heralded than...

This is all of them, then?

Mm... Yes. Of course, these are merely studies and cartoons which anticipate the finished work. Any detail or colour scheme which fails to please you can be changed or...

They're all a bit... much, don't you think? I mean, I've never worn a suit of armour in my life, and as for the ceremonial robes and capes... it's all I can do to make it through an investiture that lasts an hour. I'm scarcely interested in reminding myself of that when I'm eating my morning grapefruit.

Ah. Ah. Yes. I see. Well, as I said, anything which doesn't please you can be changed. You're looking for something less... formal then.

Formal, I could live with. All of these seem bent on... I don't know... deification? And you're sure this is all of them?

Mmm... yes. Yes, indeed. Perhaps we could discuss which of these you might most...

The reason I ask is that one of my maids told me that you had a picture submitted which you considered... unsuitable. You had a short chat with her when you arrived for our second appointment.

I'm very sorry. That was indiscreet of me.

Not at all. Not at all. Cynthia is a wonderful... conversationalist.

Ah. You are most gracious, gentle lady, but, still, I humbly apologize.

I'd like to see it, please. The unsuitable picture.

Ah. I... believe it has already been returned to the artist.

You are very sweet to be concerned about my feelings, but, like any honest man, you haven't the capacity to sustain an untruth. I am very flattered and grateful for your concern, but I'm afraid I must insist. As you are a gentleman, I am relying on you not to put me in the awkward position of having to do so more than once. Please.

As you wish, gentle lady. I have the... 'picture' is too flattering a word... the 'thing' right over this way in my office. In fact, I retained the picture for exactly the reason that I felt some comment was required when I returned it. And then I thought that even a rebuke from someone in my position might grant the... 'thing' a dignity to which it was not entitled. If you wish me to alert the appropriate authorities, I can do so at once. In fact, I should probably have done so when I first laid eyes upon it. So. Now that the wretched thing has been...

No, no. Don't cover it up again. I want to look at it.

As you wish, gentle lady. The man is obviously no better than a... beast. Insulting you, desecrating our flag. I can assure you that everyone associated with this incident within the Council will be... Ah! Ah, yes. Exactly my reaction. It is laughable. A beast, yes. But no threat to you, is it? No. A capering monkey of a thing. Ridiculous in its...

This one. This is the painter I want.

But, gentle lady... he's... well, he's not even a painter. He's... he's...

Have all the other works returned along with a cheque for twenty-five crowns and my compliments. And ask the artist... has he signed it? Ah, he has... have Mr. Zulli arrange an appointment in my suite for the day after tomorrow. Mid-evening.

Gentle lady, I must respectfully point out... in my capacity as the Chairman of...

Thank you so much. I really must return to my rooms now and write you a letter of recommendation. You've been helpful. Wonderfully helpful. Bonjour, Mr. Chairman.

You understand my situation.

I have a speculative nature. It posed no great difficulty.

I hope I won't offend you by saying that the imagery is not precisely what I was looking for. Remarkable as it is, I would have to judge it as self-pitying. I am, after all, here of my own free will. Do you understand?

Completely, my lady. Do you wish me to do some different sketches?

Is it possible for us just to discuss it?

You have my undivided attention.

What I liked about it was the portrayal of isolation and tension. But it seems to imply a tension between myself and the State which, for me, is not the larger issue. There is confinement, but this too is not the larger issue upon which your wonderful picture... speculates. I move about quite freely and (her gesture was diffidently inclusive of her living quarters) luxury itself is hardly cause for anxiety. But one feels oneself being devoured nonetheless. And not just by those with malicious intent; the effect is the same... if not greater... in the company of well-wishers. One exists on a summit of perception, surrounded by summits of lesser perception (she smiled), or more accurately: summits which are popularly perceived to be lesser. I lack no empathy with this. I remember how it was when Uncle Julius married. It seemed, for a time, as if his wife...

...had inhaled all of Palnu's air and everyone else was gasping for breath.

Thank you. The mistake is in thinking that the condition can be alleviated by the withdrawal of one's physical presence.

To remove yourself completely is to feed the hunger beyond the gilded bars until it becomes insatiable.

(she smiled at this) You're making this very easy for me. Of course, there is one... and only one... with whom this isn't the case.

Lord Julius.

And there, there the problem is one of interposing myself. I can go and see him whenever I want. He always makes time for me. But each moment that passes in his company makes me feel as if I am single-handedly holding weighty affairs of state from his attentions. I feel as if I'm a dam holding back a river... a... a...

...a distraction. A frivolous distraction.

Yes. And that's unbearable.

So you wait for him to summon you. Which he hardly ever does.

Which he never does. (remarkably, this was said without a note of bitterness)

Which he never does (the artist managed to restrain any note of surprise). Do you wish him to see the picture? (this was conversational, but direct, and caught her by surprise)

I... I'm not sure. (she sought safer ground) I know I don't want it publicly displayed. I want it to be...

Yes, yes. A personal thing (on the surface of it he was impertinent, but she was shying away from the larger issue, and here their respective roles in society did not apply). I knew that before I came here (a measured rap to her aristocratic knuckles; in spite of herself she bristled and was secretly relieved when it had no effect upon him. To him, 'here' was the leading edge of the discussion, not the luxurious confines of her suite. She misconstrued this as bravery and — as the effect this created served his purpose, he made no effort at clarification). Do you wish me to make a picture of the situation which exists between the two of you or do you wish me to make a picture of your situation relative to him?

(she pondered this for several minutes; she now understood the question but it required probing more deeply within herself than she had thought would be necessary. He was relieved that doing so came naturally to her. She accepted the necessity for an answer without entering into the needless digression of inquiring into the motive behind the question as he half expected she would — the ruler was still poised over her knuckles but she was unaware of this) I'd like it to be a picture that, if he ever came here... here to my rooms (unconsciously she had connected with his own previous distinction and had rejoined him at the leading edge of the discussion)... the picture might make him understand. (she looked at him, wondering if this was sufficient; he nodded and they were past the crisis point) May I ask you a question?

(the rap on the knuckles had obviously been too sharp; his voice reflected an aristocratic mingling of guilt and pleasure at the reversal of their roles) Certainly, my lady. What is it that you wish to know?

Two questions, really (at this assertion their roles had retreated to a more appropriate balance and they had both relaxed). Why is it you aren't taking notes?

Why is it that you don't want me to do further sketches? (at this they both smiled. Their shared purpose was now actual, the dance nearly concluded. He anticipated the final step and could afford the largesse of submission) And the other question?

Why is it that you want this commission? (her gaze was level and he felt her warmth retreating from him. She lived surrounded by sycophants and brigands, rogues and scoundrels. Her sensory apparatus quivered delicately. The smallest untruth or distortion would not go undetected)

I'm a commercial illustrator by trade. Doubtless, out of some perverse sensibility beyond my reckoning, Tarim saw fit to endow me with artistic aptitudes but has coupled these with an instinct for seeing a picture through the eyes of the inartistic — an ability to render the image in precisely the way they would do so themselves had they the skill. For many years, I have derived the greatest satisfaction from pleasing both them and myself — walking the tightrope between my patrons and my Muse. Some time ago I did the covers for a series of... reads (as enunciated by him, the word fairly dripped poison) — by a man named Victor Reid...

I've never heard of him.

You may count yourself blessed on that score, my lady. Anyway, the royalties have made me wealthy. And the wealth severed the tightrope. I had my choice of any commercial assignment I desired and that, in itself, killed all of my desire for commercial assignments.

And now you sense the hunger growing beyond your own gilded bars. (the leading edge of the discussion hurtled forward, both their scalps now tingling, their spirits buoyant)

Precisely. Now I wish only to do pictures which are intended to satisfy myself. Paintings. Not the engravings with which I have earned my livelihood. When I learned of the competition for your commission, I knew that I had found, in one, the perfect closure to my past life and the door to my future.

(she laughed delightedly as the leading edge of the discussion leapfrogged past her) So I will get a study of the painting, after all?

(suddenly he had the largest respect and admiration for her. She had transcended all of his expectations and his soul seemed to soar within his breast) Yes. You'll have the engraving in a week's time. (he now prepared the stair-step to white radiance) I'd like to have it back when I deliver the finished work.

That goes without saying. (now she felt his warmth retreat from her. The moment was lost) I'm sorry, you're right (this was insufficient and she knew it) 'I would consider it the only equitable basis for this transaction' (this was an aristocratic recitation and the foul taste in her mouth was instantaneous). We are ugly, aren't we? (the unintended meaning dragged him into the muck with her) Patrons, I mean. (the qualification reinforced the faux pas — she stood revealed to herself) I won't ask you to name your price, anyway. I know better than that, at least.

That is an awareness I have never encountered before and it pleases me more than I could ever express. Thank you. (she searched his eyes for any trace of irony and saw only sincerity. Radiance returned and he chose his moment to feed it) Perhaps you'd like to show me what clothes you want to be wearing in the picture.

(her eyes gleamed like those of a child unwrapping a longed-for gift) I didn't know how to ask. It seemed presumptuous... just to assume... assume that I could...

(the radiance between them grew and he smiled through it) But you had them picked out. Just in case.

(she blushed at this) Yes. Just in case. Did you know all along? (the obscurity of the question was intended to puncture his impenetrable self-assurance by forcing his own inquiry)

That I would get the commission? (his self-assurance thus reinforced, she was compelled merely to nod and smile) I knew that if you saw the study, no other outcome was possible.

Coming from anyone else (she teased), that would sound egotistical.

(he lost no time in reflection) Thank you.

I'll get changed and be right back. (she tugged a long, silken chord) Tell the butler I'd like a glass of wine and have him bring you whatever you want to drink or eat.

In the weeks consumed by the completion of the painting no further word regarding payment had passed between them. At last, the painter removed the engraving from its resting place on the wallpaper (of his own design) and replaced it with the finished work. He and Jaka shared a bottle of vintage red wine and sat in two armchairs facing L'Enchantement (for so he had christened it).

They sat, for the most part, in silent and separate reverie, conversing only sporadically and then lapsing into silence once more. They parted company that night, patron and artist, with a formality that was not without human warmth. They knew they would never see each other again.

A package arrived at his studio the next day which contained a small chest of solid gold, intricately carved and inlaid with precious stones. Within the box, resting on the finest purple velvet, was an eggshell adorned with a pastel flourish, painstakingly rendered in imitation of the wallpaper design which framed his picture, unmistakably rendered in an amateur's hand.

The eggshell had been broken, carefully, into two pieces.

Each night, after completing his work, he would sit contemplating the box and the eggshell halves within. He purchased some fine wood and an inexpensive set of small saws and chisels and planes. After several weeks, his hands scarred and his nails splintered, he had constructed a small, lop-sided ebony box whose lid did not fit properly. On its front was carved a relief of that same wallpaper pattern, crude but recognizable.

He lined the box with one of his best silk handkerchiefs; placed one half of the eggshell within it and had it sent, by courier, to her residence.

'SHE CAN'T POSSIBLY CHOOSE THAT WIMPY PAINTER OVER CEREBUS,' YOU THOUGHT

'CEREBUS COULD CUT HIM INTO BITE-SIZE CHUNKS WITH-OUT BREAKING A SWEAT,' YOU THOUGHT.

SHE HAD *NO* ROMANTIC INTEREST IN THE PAINTER, AND HE HAD *NO* ROMANTIC INTEREST IN *HER*.

NONE.

I'M NOT TRYING TO BE *CRUEL*, I'M TRYING TO MAKE YOU *UNDERSTAND* THAT YOU KNOW *NOTHING* ABOUT JAKA.

CEREBUS KNOWS THAT HE ~~LOVES~~ HER!

KNOWING THAT *YOU* LOVE HER ISN'T SOMETHING YOU KNOW *ABOUT HER* ...

WHAT *DO* YOU KNOW ABOUT HER-- *APART* FROM HOW SHE *LOOKS*?

LORD JULIUS' NIECE ... DANCER ... WAS MARRIED TO RICK

150

151

IT'S A STORY THAT SHE KNOWS WELL. IT BEGINS IN THE ANCIENT LIBRARY AT *LINSHIB*, WHERE TWO WOMEN, ROBED FROM HEAD TO TOE, SIT STUDYING RESEARCH MATERIALS... ONE OF THEM IS NAMED *CIRIN*. THE OTHER IS *SERNA*. CIRIN WRITES COPIOUS PAGES UPON COPIOUS PAGES.... SERNA OFFERS COMMENTS AND QUESTIONS. CIRIN IS A SCHOLAR OF ANCIENT MATRIARCHAL SOCIETIES, *GODDESS* WORSHIP AND REVOLUTION -- AT THE END OF EACH DAY, CIRIN *DESTROYS* ALL SHE HAS WRITTEN AND BEGINS EACH DAY ANEW, REFINING AND DISTILLING HER PROGRAM

AT LAST, WITH TREMBLING HAND, SHE INSCRIBES A SINGLE SHEET OF PAPER -- WHICH WILL NOT BE DESTROYED AT DAY'S END -- WITH '*THE FIVE CORNER-STONES*': COMMUNAL SAFETY. THE SHARING OF RESOURCES. HARD LABOUR FROM SUNRISE TO SUNSET. QUARTERLY FEST-IVALS (LASTING THREE DAYS) OF EXCESS AND DEBAUCHERY. ASCETICISM IN ALL AREAS OF EXISTENCE.

TIME IS OF THE ESSENCE

THE HUNDRED YEARS' OCCUPATION OF THEIR NATIVE UPPER FELDA IS COMING TO AN *END*. AS THE SEPRAN LEGIONS WITHDRAW, THEY ARE EXECUTING ALL MALES BE-TWEEN THE AGES OF FIVE AND FORTY.

SOON, UPPER FELDA WILL BE A COUNTRY COMPOSED ALMOST *EXCLUSIVELY* OF OLD MEN, INFANT BOYS, GIRLS, YOUNG WOMEN ...

... AND *MOTHERS*.

152

153

AH!

CIRIN AND SERNA INTRODUCE THEIR *REVOLUTION* WITHIN THEIR RURAL COMMUNITY OF RIVERSIDE — THE WEEKLY *QUILTING CIRCLE* THEY HAD PARTICIPATED IN SINCE YOUNG ADULTHOOD. MOTHERS, YOUNG AND OLD. MOST ARE RECENTLY *WIDOWED*, THEIR HUSBANDS EXECUTED BY THE SEPRAN LEGIONS WHICH HAVE BEEN RECALLED TO SHORE UP A CRUMBLING EMPIRE.

FEAR OF THE FUTURE, MOST PARTICULARLY, THEIR *CHILDREN'S* FUTURE PROVIDES THEIR MOTIVE IN EMBRACING THE 'FIVE CORNERSTONES'

THE GREATEST HURDLE? PERSUADING EVERYONE TO WEAR THE ROBES, BUT CIRIN IS *INSISTENT* — ASCETIC LIVING CAN ALLOW FOR NO VANITY AND NO INTRUSION BY VANITY'S *DISTINCTIONS:* WHO IS ATTRACTIVE AND WHO IS PLAIN? WHOSE HAIR IS LONGEST, THE MOST STYLISH? WHO HAS THE BEST COMPLEXION? THE NICEST CLOTHES?

THE MOST ATTRACTIVE OF THEM, THE ONES WITH THE LONGEST OR THE MOST STYLISH HAIR, THE BEST COMPLEXIONS, THE NICEST CLOTHES ARE THE LAST TO CAPITULATE

A NEW *AWARENESS* OVERTAKES THEM NOW, INSULATED WITHIN THEIR ROBES, ALL ANXIETY ABOUT THEIR *APPEARANCES* SUBSIDES. WITH NO *COSMETIC BASIS* UPON WHICH TO JUDGE ONE ANOTHER THEIR ATTENTIONS MOVE QUICKLY FROM SURFACE ISSUES TO ISSUES OF *SUBSTANCE.*

THEY ARE NOW *EQUALS.*

AND IT IS *AS EQUALS* THAT THEIR *REAL WORK* BEGINS.

154

THIS IS *COMMUNAL SAFETY* WHICH IS SERNA'S JURISDICTION (*CIRIN* CHOOSES TO REMAIN IGNORANT OF THE DETAILS). COMMITTING VIOLENCE AGAINST A WOMAN -- _ANY_ VIOLENCE, _ANY_ WOMAN -- IS PUNISHABLE BY SWIFT EXECUTION,

THESE EXECUTIONS ARE CARRIED OUT BY SERNA UNDER COVER OF NIGHT-- THE ACCUSED'S THROAT IS CUT.

AFTER SEVERAL HUSBANDS AND FATHERS AND GRAND-FATHERS HAVE DIED, ABUSE GOES UNREPORTED FOR A TIME.

ROBES AND HOODS EFFECTIVELY CONCEAL CUTS AND BRUISES

AND THEN A *QUIET-NATURED* MOTHER MENTIONS OCCASIONAL SLAPS AND PUNCHES ADMINISTERED BY HER HUSBAND OF TWENTY YEARS

HE IS FOUND WITH HIS THROAT CUT...

AT THE NEXT *QUILTING CIRCLE* EVERYONE WAITS TO HEAR WHAT SHE WILL SAY.

SHE DISCUSSES A SWEATER SHE IS KNITTING AND A FAMILY OF RABBITS SHE FOUND THAT MORNING.

SEVERAL MORE PERPETRATORS ARE IDENTIFIED AND EXECUTED

THE MEN GROW OLDER. THE MEN DRINK. THE MEN DIE.

SOON, EVEN THE TAVERN BECOMES FREE FROM VIOLENCE.

SERNA TRAINS HER SISTERHOOD OF ASSASSINS IN SECRET--CALLING THEM 'CIRINISTS', AN HOMAGE TO THE MASTERMIND OF THE REVOLUTION. SHE SELECTS THE BIGGEST AND THE STRONGEST OF THE WOMEN FOR *INDUCTION*...

THE BOYS, LIKE THEIR FATHERS AND GRAND-FATHERS DRINK AND OCCUPY THEIR TIME WITH SPORT AND RECREATIONS.

WHEN THEY REACH YOUNG MANHOOD THEY ARE CHOSEN BY THEIR *LIFE-MATES* FOR PURPOSES OF *PROCREATION*...

IN THE FIFTH YEAR, LOWER FELDA ATTEMPTS AN INVASION OF ITS EASTERN NEIGHBOUR, SEIZING LAND BUT FINDING THAT THE ONLY FOOD STORES ARE THOSE SET ASIDE FOR THE *QUARTERLY FESTIVALS*...

THEY ATTEMPT TO IMPOSE TAXATION AND FIND THAT UPPER FELDA HAS NO *CURRENCY* OR PRECIOUS METALS. BUILDINGS AND RESIDENCES TO HOUSE THE *OCCUPATIONAL GOVERNMENT* MUST BE CONSTRUCTED FROM MATERIALS IMPORTED AT *PROHIBITIVE* EXPENSE.

SOLDIERS ATTEMPTING TO PRESS THE MOTHERS INTO SERVICE ARE FOUND WITH THEIR THROATS CUT.

THE NUMBER OF MERCENARIES IS *DOUBLED*, AS IS THE DURATION OF EACH TOUR OF DUTY. THE CASUALTIES QUADRUPLE.

INSIDE OF A YEAR, FIFTY PER-CENT OF THE *GROSS DOMESTIC PRODUCT* OF LOWER FELDA IS REQUIRED TO SUPPORT AND MAINTAIN THE *TOTTERING* OCCUPATIONAL REGIME.

FRUSTRATION REACHES THE BOILING POINT IN *LOWER FELDA.* A MILITARY COUP DISPLACES THE *OLIGARCHY.* THE LARGEST MILITARY FORCE IN LOWER FELDAN HISTORY IS MOUNTED WHICH ONLY ESCALATES THE CASUALTY RATE. AFTER TWO YEARS THE ORDER IS GIVEN FOR *LOWER FELDAN* FORCES TO WITHDRAW

ALL LOWER FELDAN CIVILIANS IN THE OCCUPIED TERRITORIES ARE ALSO ORDERED TO RETURN HOME.

A NETWORK OF FORTRESSES, CONNECTED BY STONE WALLS TWO METERS THICK AND SEVEN METERS HIGH, IS CONSTRUCTED BY THE *LOWER FELDANS* ALONG THE BORDER — *THE GREAT IRON BARRIER*

IN THE FARMING COMMUNITIES OF *LOWER FELDA* -- REPRESENTING EIGHTY PERCENT OF ITS TERRITORY ...

REPATRIATED LOWER FELDAN MOTHERS DON ROBES AND HOODS AND FORM *QUILTING CIRCLES.*

COMMERCE IN THE SMALL VILLAGES AND TOWNS BEGINS TO SUFFER.

URBAN ECONOMIES RAVAGED BY THE BURDEN OF MILITARY MISADVENTURE DECLINE EVEN *MORE* RAPIDLY.

THE *LOWER FELDAN* MILITARY DICTATORSHIP (HUMILIATED BY UPPER FELDA) ARE THE FIRST TO MYTHOLOGIZE THE 'CIRINISTS' AS A RACE OF BLOODTHIRSTY AMAZONS, NOCTURNAL DEMONESSES HUNTING, DISEMBOWELING AND DEVOURING THEIR HUMAN PREY.

CIRIN IS REPUTED TO BE THOUSANDS OF YEARS OLD, CAPABLE OF TRANSFORMING HERSELF INTO ANY PREDATORY ANIMAL OR BIRD, RENDERING HERSELF *INVISIBLE* AND ROAMING THE MOONLIT FELDWAR COUNTRYSIDE AS A DISEMBODIED SHADOW.

READS PUBLISHERS SEIZE ON THIS NEW DEMONIZED FOE (HAVING *EXHAUSTED* THE HSIFANS' POTENTIAL SOME TIME BEFORE), MANY LONG-OUT-OF-PRINT READS DEALING WITH MATRIMONY AND MOTHERHOOD ARE CREDITED TO CIRIN AND (WITH THE ADDITION OF *LURID* COVERS AND ILLUSTRATIONS AND THE APPENDING OF BLOODY RETRIBUTION TO THEIR HOMEMAKER HOMILIES) DOMINATE THE BEST-SELLER LISTS.

THE *QUILTING CIRCLES* SPREAD THROUGHOUT LOWER FELDA AND THE RURAL AREAS OF IEST -- *HOODS* AND *ROBES* MORE EFFECTIVE THAN *SHIELDS* AND *SWORDS* IN MAINTAINING SAFETY...

SERNA FINDS HERSELF *NEARLY OVERWHELMED* BY APPLICANTS TO THE 'SECRET' SISTERHOOD — EACH QUILTING CIRCLE SOON BOASTS AT LEAST A HALF DOZEN 'COMMUNAL SAFETY OFFICERS'

THE NAME CHANGE IS NECESSARY: 'CIRINIST' BECOMES THE UNIVERSAL DESIGNATION FOR THE *HOODED* AND ROBED WOMEN

DESPITE CIRIN'S OBJECTIONS

MONSTER MOTHERS of UPPER FELDA

CIRIN IS CONCERNED BY THE INCREASING *MILITANCY* OF SERNA'S SISTERHOOD... IN AN ATTEMPT TO REAWAKEN HER MOVEMENT'S HARMONIOUS FOUNDATION, *COMMUNAL SAFETY OFFICERS* ARE EXCUSED FROM THE *QUILTING CIRCLE* GATHERINGS...

THE RESOURCES ARE STILL DIVIDED EQUALLY, BUT NOW THE *COMMUNAL SAFEY OFFICERS* DEPART BEFORE THE ACTUAL *QUILTING* BEGINS.

SOON— ONLY A COMMUNAL SAFETY 'DELEGATE' ATTENDS, REQUISITIONING *TEN* PERCENT OF THE RESOURCES.

THEN *FIFTEEN* PERCENT.

THEN *TWENTY*

THEN *TWENTY-FIVE.*

ONE NIGHT, CIRIN AWAKENS TO THE SOUND OF FOOTSTEPS INSIDE HER MODEST DWELLING.

LIES
LIES
LIES
LIES
LIES
LIES

162

164

SERNA – AS YOU CAN HEAR – IS UNABLE TO ACKNOWLEDGE HER PAST. IT IS THE COMMONEST OF MISAPPREHENSIONS THAT AN ACT OF *BAD FAITH* DID NOT TAKE PLACE IF IT WENT UNNOTICED.

SHE INHERITED *CIRIN'S* METICULOUSLY CRAFTED MOVEMENT SO THOROUGHLY IN TUNE WITH HUMAN NATURE AND HUMAN IDEALS...

...AND GRAFTED ONTO IT A WAR MACHINE WHICH HAD ABSOLUTE TOLERANCE FOR THE FREE EXPRESSION OF IDEAS AND A BRUTAL *INTOLERANCE* OF ANY ACTION TAKEN OUTSIDE OF CLEARLY DEFINED PARAMETERS.

AGAIN, THOROUGHLY IN TUNE WITH HUMAN NATURE AND HUMAN IDEALS.

THE *QUILTING CIRCLES* ARE THE ENGINE WHICH DRIVES THE MOVEMENT, WEAKENING AND MAKING VULNERABLE EACH OLIGARCHY, EACH DICTATORSHIP, EACH URBAN CENTER, EACH SYSTEM OF GOVERNMENT...

COUNTRY AFTER COUNTRY FALLS TO THEM -- VIRTUALLY WITHOUT BLOODSHED. INTO THE POWER VACUUM STEPS THE FORMER SERNA AND HER COMMUNAL SAFETY OFFICERS

THEY ARE MORE *FEARED* THAN RESPECTED, BUT A CONSENSUS PREVAILS! 'SAFETY FIRST', 'ONLY THE VIOLENT ARE PUNISHED'!

IN ANY ENVIRONMENT, THE SYSTEM WHICH IS THE MOST TOLERANT OF *DISSENT*, WHICHEVER SYSTEM *BEST MIRRORS* HUMAN NATURE WILL *FLOURISH*, HOWEVER IMPERFECT IT MIGHT BE.

THE *LEAST IMPERFECT* SYSTEM WINS -- SO TO SPEAK

WHICH IS WHY YOU COULD NEVER CONQUER *ESTARCION*.

168

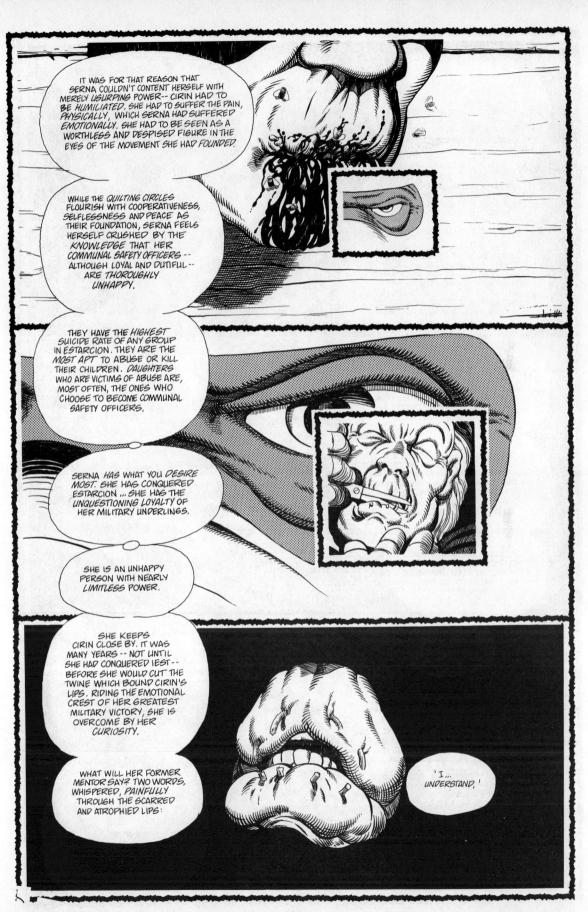

IT WAS FOR THAT REASON THAT SERNA COULDN'T CONTENT HERSELF WITH MERELY *USURPING* POWER-- CIRIN HAD TO BE *HUMILIATED*. SHE HAD TO SUFFER THE PAIN, *PHYSICALLY*, WHICH SERNA HAD SUFFERED *EMOTIONALLY*. SHE HAD TO BE SEEN AS A WORTHLESS AND DESPISED FIGURE IN THE EYES OF THE MOVEMENT SHE HAD *FOUNDED*.

WHILE THE *QUILTING CIRCLES* FLOURISH WITH COOPERATIVENESS, SELFLESSNESS AND PEACE AS THEIR FOUNDATION, SERNA FEELS HERSELF CRUSHED BY THE *KNOWLEDGE* THAT HER COMMUNAL SAFETY OFFICERS -- ALTHOUGH LOYAL AND DUTIFUL-- ARE *THOROUGHLY UNHAPPY*.

THEY HAVE THE *HIGHEST* SUICIDE RATE OF ANY GROUP IN ESTARCION. THEY ARE THE *MOST APT* TO ABUSE OR KILL THEIR CHILDREN. *DAUGHTERS* WHO ARE VICTIMS OF ABUSE ARE, MOST OFTEN, THE ONES WHO CHOOSE TO BECOME COMMUNAL SAFETY OFFICERS.

SERNA *HAS* WHAT YOU *DESIRE MOST*. SHE HAS CONQUERED ESTARCION ... SHE HAS THE *UNQUESTIONING* LOYALTY OF HER MILITARY UNDERLINGS.

SHE IS AN UNHAPPY PERSON WITH NEARLY *LIMITLESS* POWER.

SHE KEEPS CIRIN CLOSE BY. IT WAS MANY YEARS -- NOT UNTIL SHE HAD CONQUERED IEST-- BEFORE SHE WOULD CUT THE TWINE WHICH BOUND CIRIN'S LIPS. RIDING THE EMOTIONAL CREST OF HER GREATEST MILITARY VICTORY, SHE IS OVERCOME BY HER *CURIOSITY*.

WHAT WILL HER FORMER MENTOR SAY? TWO WORDS, WHISPERED, *PAINFULLY* THROUGH THE SCARRED AND ATROPHIED LIPS:

'I... UNDERSTAND.'

SERNA, *ENRAGED*, BEATS CIRIN INTO UNCONSCIOUSNESS. SHE DOES *NOT*, HOWEVER, HAVE CIRIN'S LIPS SEWN SHUT AGAIN. IT IS ONE OF THOSE DECISIONS A CREATION MAKES WHICH IS *INEXPLICABLE* EVEN TO HER (OR HIS) CREATOR...

INSTEAD A GUARD-STENOGRAPHER IS ASSIGNED. EACH NIGHT, A FULL TRANSCRIPT OF CIRIN'S WORDS IS BROUGHT TO SERNA

CIRIN RECITES POETRY FOR THE MOST PART, REMINISCES ABOUT THE EARLY DAYS OF THE MOVEMENT, ATTEMPTS TO ENGAGE THE *GUARD-STENOGRAPHER* IN CONVERSATION AND (REBUFFED) REMINISCES ABOUT HER FRIENDS AND THEIR CHILDREN

CREATORS CAN ONLY *OBSERVE* ACTIONS AND *HEAR* WORDS. WHAT GOES THROUGH SERNA'S MIND AS SHE PORES OVER THE TRANSCRIPTS? SHE OCCASIONALLY HURLS THEM AWAY FROM HER (BUT ALWAYS *RETRIEVES* THEM) AND OFTEN MUTTERS 'LIES' OR 'MADNESS' (BUT CONTINUES READING)

THE UNMISTAKABLE IMPRESSION I'M LEFT WITH IS THAT SHE HAS, *INDEED*, CONVINCED HERSELF THAT SHE *IS* CIRIN. HER PRODIGIOUS TELEPATHIC ABILITIES WERE TURNED INWARD AND REMOVED ALL MEMORY OF HER 'COUP' WHICH *DID* -- I CAN ASSURE YOU -- TAKE PLACE

EVEN AFTER THE *REAL* CIRIN HAD HER LITTLE 'CHAT' WITH YOU, SERNA DID NOT ORDER CIRIN'S LIPS *RESEALED* (AS I HAD EXPECTED SHE WOULD)

OF COURSE, ONCE I'VE RETURNED SERN THE

YAAWN

SORRY.

FORGOT WHO I WAS DEALING WITH HERE.

SKTCHA SKTCH

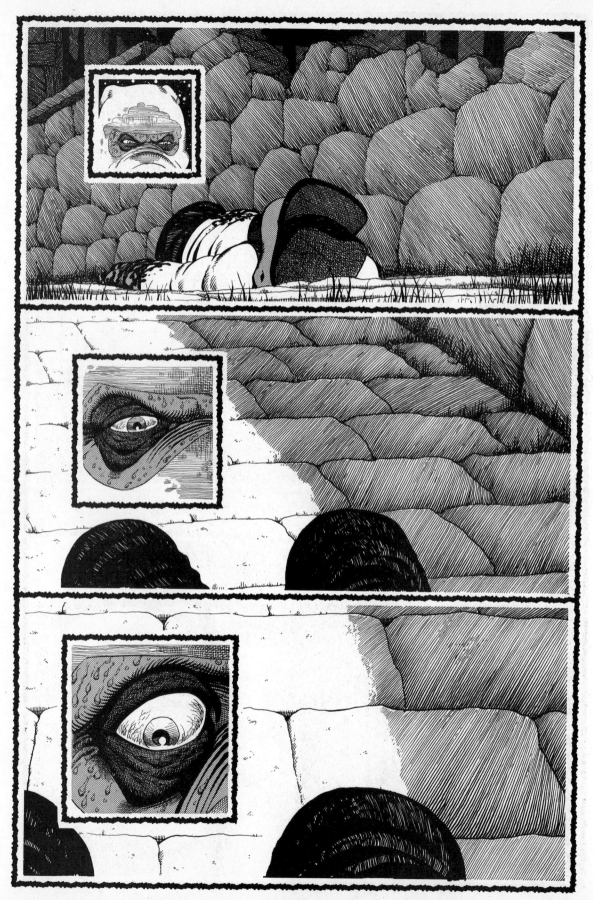

175

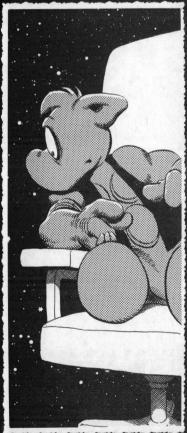

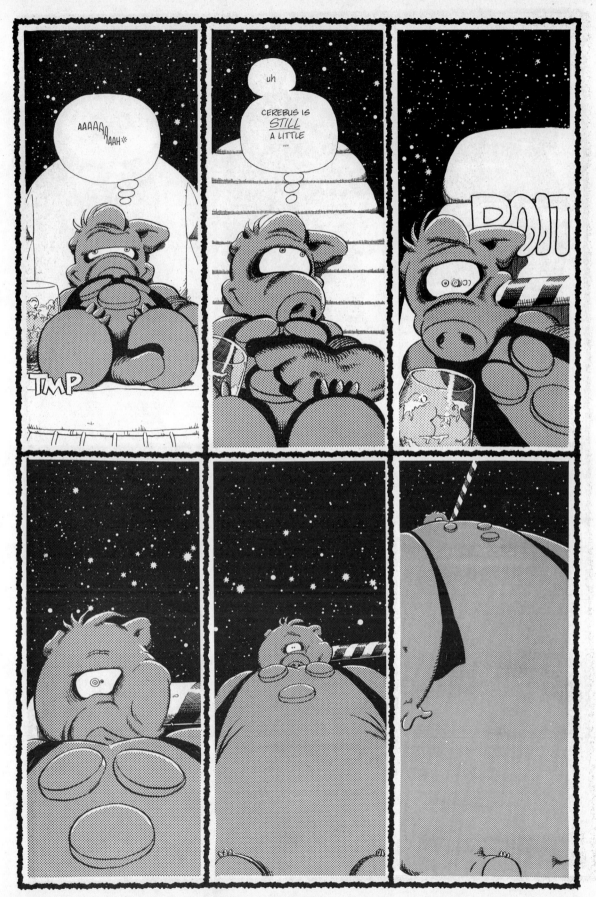

OF COURSE, WHAT *HE* SAW, YOUR *MUTUAL* AARDVARKIAN ANCESTORS *ALSO* SAW. HE PREVAILED UPON HIS ARTISANS AND SCULPTORS TO RENDER YOUR IMAGE IN EVERY IMAGINABLE MEDIUM.

THOUGH NOT *ALL* OF THE PIGTS BELIEVED IN THE PROPHECY OF YOUR COMING, *ENOUGH* DID

TO MAINTAIN THAT BELIEF FOR A PERIOD OF TIME

THOUGH NOT *ALL* OF THE AARDVARKIAN ANCESTORS BELIEVED YOUR FORM TO BE THE IDEAL (OF WHICH THEY THEMSELVES HAD BEEN *FLAWED* MANIFESTATIONS) *ENOUGH* DID...

TO IMBUE THE ICONS WITH THEIR COLLECTIVE SPIRIT, PROVIDING FOCUS FOR THE BELIEFS OF GENERATIONS OF PIGTS.

HOWEVER, BELIEF BEGAN TO WAVER. DOUBT BEGAN TO SPREAD. THE SHAMAN - KING CRAFTED MEDALLIONS, A HELMET AND A SHORT SWORD OF HARD, GRAY METAL ...

HE CALLED HIS PEOPLE TO HIM WITHOUT *FIRST* COMMUNING WITH HIS ANCESTORS.

'THESE WILL BE HIS,' HE TOLD THEM.

SUICIDE KILLS NOT ONLY THE *BODY* BUT THE *SOUL* AS WELL -- LEAVING THE AARDVARKIAN ANCESTORS TO WONDER IF THE SHAMAN-KING'S FINAL GESTURE HAD BEEN ONE OF PROFOUND *BRAVERY* OR EXTREME *COWARDICE*, A PROTRACTED CIVIL WAR BETWEEN PIGTISH TRIBES MIRRORS THIS CONFLICT

MUCH BLOOD IS SPILLED OVER THE CENTURIES AS ONE FACTION AND ANOTHER CLAIMS POSSESSION OF THE SHAMAN-KING'S REMAINS, THE HELMET, THE SWORD AND THE MEDALLIONS ... SOON THESE ARTIFACTS ARE LOST AND CONSIDERED *MYTHICAL*

WHICH IS PERHAPS WHAT THE SHAMAN-KING HAD INTENDED.

A FACTION OF THE PIGTS WENT UNDERGROUND -- *LITERALLY* -- AND KEPT ALIVE THE ICON OF '*HE WHO IS TO COME AFTER*'

THEY WERE PROTECTED BY THE SPIRITS OF THOSE ANCESTORS WHO BELIEVED IN THAT ICON ABOVE ALL OTHERS -- THE PERFECT AARDVARKIAN FORM.

AND IT WAS YOU WHO FOUND THE MEDALLIONS, HELMET AND THE SWORD IN YOUR TRAVELS.

HAD YOU BEEN IN POSSESSION OF ALL THREE WHEN YOU MET THE *PIGTS*...

POIT!

THEY WOULD HAVE *TRANSMUTED* INTO *SOLID GOLD* BEFORE YOUR VERY EYES.

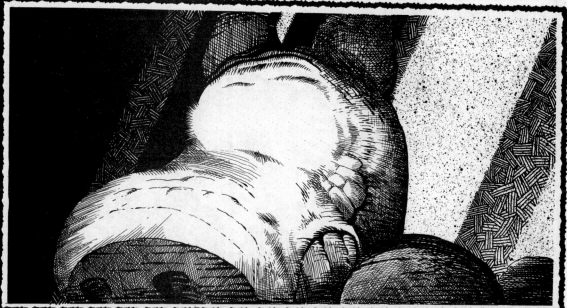

192

194

'THE CRAWLER'-- MISSHAPEN AND RAVENOUS-- A MANIFESTATION OF THE AIMLESS, PLODDING FUTURE BEFORE YOU

THE 'LAST RULER OF A DYING RACE' -- A BUMBLING, YET ARROGANT BUFFOON.

A MANIFESTATION OF YOUR SELF-DECEPTION, INCOMPETENCE AND BLUSTER

TURG, THE IGNORANT NORTHERN BARBARIAN YOU WOULD ALWAYS BE.

'THE BROTHERS OF THE BLACK SUN'

A DISPLACED TRIBE OF HERETICAL PIGTS...

THEIR INSIGNIA: A STYLISED, INVERTED AARDVARK HEAD

MANIFESTATION OF YOUR DESTINY TURNED UPSIDE-DOWN.

SINCE CEREBUS WAS COMPLETELY UNAWARE OF THE 'IBOGUS DEATH' MANIFESTATION, I CAN'T SEE ANY GOOD REASON TO BRING THE MATTER UP, SO I WON'T...

195

GONE.

YOUR OBSESSIVE INTEREST IN GOLD AND THE *CHAOTIC INFLUENCE* YOU HAVE ON PEOPLE AND EVENTS SERVE YOU IN GOOD STEAD IN THE FIELD OF *POLITICS*...

AND ARE EVEN *BETTER-SUITED* TO THE CHURCH -- FOUNDED AS IT IS ON *PROPHECY* AND *MONEY*

HAVING FRACTURED YOUR *PIGTISH* DESTINY, YOU DRIFT INTO THE VORTEX OF THE *EASTERN* CHURCH -- AS HAD SO MANY OF YOUR ANCESTORS BEFORE YOU...

MAN VERSUS WOMAN, RULER VERSUS REBEL, RICH VERSUS POOR, CAPTOR VERSUS CAPTIVE, AARDVARK VERSUS HUMAN, ETCETERA

FIRST ONE AND THEN THE OTHER

TWO *INCARNATIONS* LOCKED INTO AN *ENDLESS, POINTLESS* DUALITY

BUT, OF COURSE, THAT WOULD COME LATER. *FIRST*, YOUR SUCCESS AS POPE (COUPLED WITH THE NEAR-CONSENSUS THAT YOU REPRESENTED THE *IDEAL* FORM OF THE AARDVARK)

CALLED FORTH THE *CLOSEST MANIFESTATION* OF THE *FULFILLED* PROPHECY.

GUESS WHO?

BRAN MAC MUFIN RECOGNIZED THE *NATURE* OF THE MANIFESTATION

YOUR DESTRUCTION OF THE PIGTISH IDOL HAD CALLED FORTH A TRAVESTY OF THAT IDOL IN *HUMAN* FORM.

HAVING CHOSEN TO HAVE FAITH IN *YOU*-- INSTEAD OF THE *ICON* -- BRAN SAW SUICIDE AS THE ONLY *HONOURABLE* RECOURSE OPEN TO HIM...

IN THE ABSENCE OF THE *GENUINE* IDOL, IS IT POSSIBLE THAT *NECROSSI/THRUNK* MIGHT HAVE FULFILLED SOME *PART* OF YOUR FRACTURED DESTINY?

THERE'S NO WAY OF KNOWING, REALLY...

IS THERE?

A BIT *LONG-WINDED* AS ANSWERS GO, BUT THERE YOU HAVE IT...

THAT'S

'EXACTLY'

WHAT THOSE 'DAMNED THINGS' ARE.

201

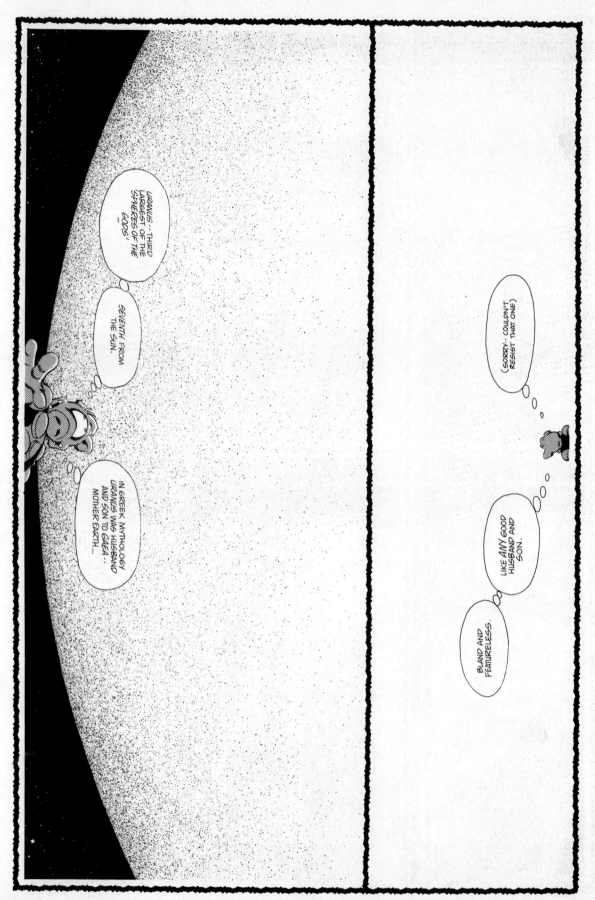

YOU COULD *MAKE* JAKA LOVE CEREBUS *'THAT'* WAY!

I DON'T SUPPOSE YOU'RE INTERESTED IN *HEARING* ABOUT HOW THE *SHAMAN-KING'S* MISTAKE WAS IN SEEKING THE IDEAL AARDVARKIAN *'FORM'* WITH NO REGARD FOR THE IDEAL *'NATURE'*--? A MISTAKE GROUNDED IN HIS BLIND BELIEF IN *ICONOLATRY*...?

NAY.

OR HOW THAT *SCHISM* BETWEEN *SURFACE* NATURE AND *SUBSTANTIAL* NATURE IMPLIED THE INEVITABILITY OF THE CONFLICT BETWEEN YOURSELF AND *SERNA*-- LOCKING THE TWO OF YOU INTO A FRUITLESS ATTEMPT TO DETERMINE WHETHER *MALENESS* IS A NATURE OF *SUBSTANCE* WHILE *FEMALENESS* IS A NATURE OF *SURFACE* OR *VICE-VERSA?* INEVITABLY YOUR RESPECTIVE GENDERS-- YOUR GENITALIA-- BECAME ICONS TO YOU, OBSCURING

THE...uh... LARGER CONTEXT OF...uh AARDVARKIAN....uh

AARDVARKIAN *NATURE*-- INCLUDING THE...*LARGEST*... UNRESOLVED QUESTION OF WHETHER TWO AARDVARKS CAN PRODUCE AARDVARK OFF-SPRING. ARE...uh... ARE AARDVARKS *POTENTIAL MUTATIONS?* OR

IS THE *HISTORICAL* PERCEPTION OF THEMSELVES AS... uh SPONTANEOUSLY

GENERATED

ABBERATIONS ...uh...

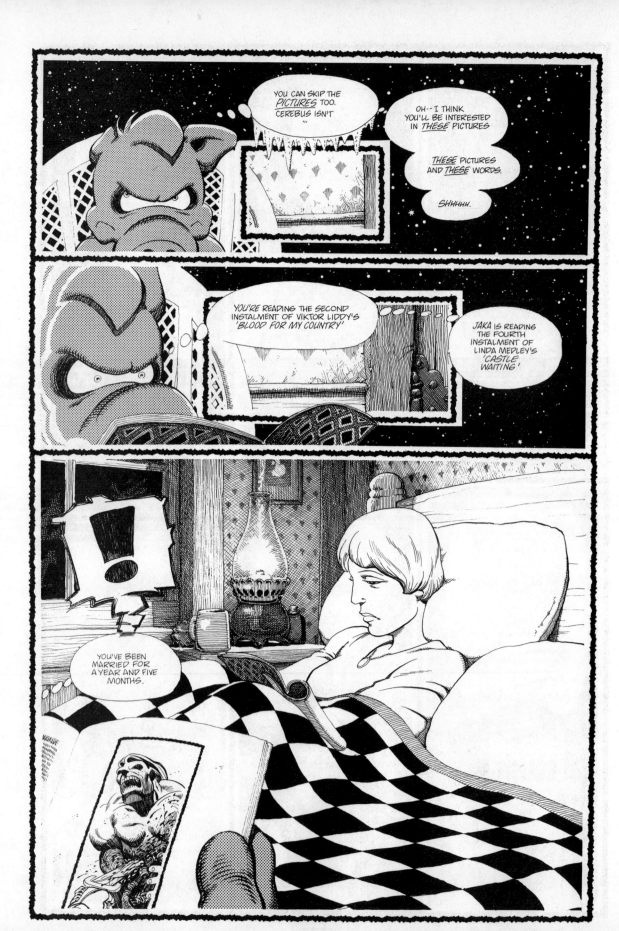

SHE LOOKS SO--_SO_...

UNHAPPY?

NAY-- _UGLY._

SHE CUT OFF HER _HAIR_-- WHY DID SHE CUT OFF HER HAIR?

YOU TOLD HER TO. YOU TOLD HER ONLY _SLUTS_ AND _HARLOTS_ HAVE LONG HAIR

IT MAKES HER LOOK LIKE AN UGLY, SKINNY _BOY!_

MM. YOU TOLD HER THAT WHEN SHE CAME BACK FROM GETTING IT _CUT._

WHICH MADE HER _CRY._

NOT RIGHT _THEN,_ OF COURSE. IF SHE CRIES WHEN YOU'RE AROUND YOU YELL AT HER AND THREATEN TO _HIT_ HER... BUT WHEN YOU'RE _NOT_ AROUND SHE CRIES QUITE A BIT...

THAT'S WHERE SHE GOT THE POUCHES UNDER HER EYES

FROM CRYING AND NOT GETTING ENOUGH _SLEEP._

YOU TOLD HER IT'S HER '_DUTY_' TO KEEP YOU COMPANY AT NIGHT-- SHE ISN'T _ALLOWED_ TO SLEEP UNTIL YOU'RE FINISHED _READING,_ EVEN THOUGH _SHE_ HAS TO WORK IN THE MORNING AND YOU _DON'T_...

JUST ONE OF YOUR MANY _RULES_

LIKE 'NO TALKING AFTER DINNER' (TALKING AFTER DINNER GIVES YOU INDIGESTION)

NOT VERY... *SATISFYING* WAS IT. SHUT UP.

A LOT LIKE *SOPHIA*

BEFORE *SHE* LEFT YOU.

SHE WAS 'THERE'

BUT SHE WASN'T REALLY '*THERE*'

JAKA IS ALREADY *PLANNING* HOW SHE'S GOING TO *LEAVE* YOU -- THREE MONTHS, MAYBE FOUR -- LESS THAN A YEAR CERTAINLY...

I *CAN* MAKE HER LOVE YOU -- BUT I *CAN'T* MAKE HER LOVE *STRONGER* THAN HER NEED TO BE *HAPPY*... OR HER INSTINCT FOR SELF-PRESERVATION

THE *HAIR*.

EXCUSE ME?

IT WAS THE *HAIR*. --YOU JUST HAVE TO PUT JAKA'S *HAIR* BACK THE WAY IT WAS...

CEREBUS *KNOWS* THAT CUTTING HER HAIR WILL MAKE HER *UGLY*, SO CEREBUS WON'T TELL HER TO CUT IT OFF THIS TIME.

MM. ANYTHING *ELSE?*

AYE -- YOU JUST HAVE TO MAKE HER *HAPPY* TO BE WITH CEREBUS *NO MATTER WHAT.*

NO MATTER WHAT.

AYE. *NO MATTER WHAT.*

210

SWEETIE?

IT'S OKAY, JAKA.

CEREBUS IS RIGHT HERE

GO BACK TO SLEEP

MMMMMM

OKAY!-- YOU MAKE HER *HAPPY* TO STAY WITH CEREBUS *NO* MATTER WHAT

AND YOU MAKE IT SO CEREBUS NEVER HITS HER AGAIN--*EVER*

OR *THREATENS* TO HIT HER?

AYE.

AYE, THAT'S A GOOD ONE.

IF SHE'S GOING TO BE HAPPY TO STAY WITH CEREBUS *NO MATTER WHAT,* CEREBUS WON'T *NEED* TO HIT HER-- *OR* THREATEN TO HIT HER

IT'S A *DEAL.*

YOU AND JAKA HAVE BEEN MARRIED FOR TWO YEARS. THINGS ARE GOING VERY WELL FOR BOTH OF YOU.

YOU SPEND YOUR DAYS READING BLOODTHIRSTY TALES OF MILITARY MAYHEM ANTICIPATING JAKA'S RETURN FROM HER JOB.

YOU HAVE LITTLE ON YOUR MIND BESIDES YOUR EVENING MEAL-- JAKA HAS BECOME SOMETHING OF A *GOURMET COOK*.

THAT CHANGES THIS *PARTICULAR* DAY, FOR THIS IS THE DAY YOU SEE YOUR NEW NEIGHBOUR FOR THE FIRST TIME.

THE HOT SUMMER SUDDENLY SEEMS A LOT *HOTTER*.

A *LOT* HOTTER.

SHE FINISHES HANGING OUT HER WASH.

AND GOES BACK INSIDE HER HOUSE

YOU DON YOUR HEAVY BLUE SWEATER (THE ONE JAKA HAS SAID MAKES YOU LOOK THINNER) AND STROLL OUTSIDE

WHISTLING VERY LOUDLY, YOU SCUFF A FEW STRAY LEAVES INTO A PILE -- YOU GRIP THE TRUNK OF THE SAPLING, SHAKING IT *SLIGHTLY* (AS IF TESTING ITS SOLIDITY).

AT A LOSS FOR ANY *FURTHER* ACTIVITY, YOU RETREAT INSIDE, BATHED IN SWEAT

YOU REPEAT THIS RITUAL OVER THE COURSE OF SEVERAL DAYS, NOT DARING -- EVEN *BRIEFLY* -- TO LOOK AT THE HOUSE NEXT DOOR.

ON THE *SIXTH* DAY, THE SOUND OF THE DOOR OPENING BEHIND YOU MAKES YOU *JUMP.*

JAKA HAS COME HOME EARLY FOR SOME REASON.

I'm sorry I'm so nosy, but aren't you hot in that sweater?

(Your throat has gone dry and clutches at your words) Nay (coughing). Nay, Cerebus has spent a lot of time in the southlands. Cerebus doesn't get hot like most people.

You're lucky. I've never been outside of Palnu. My name's Joanne. (an awkward silence) I guess we're neighbours.

Cerebus is married (this is said too quickly).

(she misses the implication) Hey, me too. (another awkward silence) Fred — he's my husband — Fred isn't around much. He travels a lot on business. (another awkward silence) I get lonesome sometimes. Fred doesn't like me to (she gropes for an explanation) He loves me a lot, you know? He likes me to (Fred's will asserts itself in his absence) I just spend too much time with my old friends, talking a lot of foolishness instead of taking care of my responsibilities.

(this is a very familiar refrain and you muse aloud) Aye... Jaka's the same way (Joanne seems to shrink within herself, as if Fred himself has caught her in a major transgression) (her withdrawal apparent, you scramble mentally to recover lost ground) Uh... she doesn't... she doesn't like Cerebus... talking to people when she's at work.

(her eyes widen at this. The blatant lie has reinforced the tenuous connection. She glances over her shoulder as if Fred might manifest himself in the kitchen at any moment) Well, maybe we shouldn't be talking then.

(quickly) Nay. Cerebus wants to talk to you.

(for several moments she wrestles inwardly with this; a long-suppressed fire reaches her eyes) I don't think it's fair (she starts at the unexpected edge in her own voice). I mean, it's just... (barely a whisper) talking.

Aye. It doesn't mean (you're quoting Jaka now and feel a twinge of guilt as you do so) you love him any less. (you can't help yourself; Jaka's words are your best weapon) After all, you're his wife, not his prisoner.

(melting at this, she smiles. Seeing her smile, you melt in turn) I guess we've got a lot in common, huh?

(at first you think she's referring to herself and Jaka; it takes you a moment to merge with the lie) Aye. (the answer is suited to both interpretations; a mixture of shame and exhilaration rises within you)

As long as we get our responsibilities taken care of (she is unused to making the rules for herself and pauses to choose her words carefully) we could talk some more (unexpectedly, she has found herself outside Fred's prison; her vertiginous reaction begs the security of qualification:) Maybe. (it's okay to be outside the cage, isn't it?)

(there is a stirring in your groin) Cerebus would like that.

(afraid of losing the small victory) Well, okay.

(afraid of losing the small victory) Okay.

(smiling her relief and her gratitude) 'Bye.

(smiling from your groin) 'Bye.

SHE IS RETICENT AT FIRST, listening and smiling. Soon, however, her thin trickle of comment becomes a mighty stream of observation and then a raging torrent of confession. She pours forth the story of her twenty (be still, your throbbing groin) summers of existence. Frequently she edges around her subject, cautious and restrained at its perimeter — the truth straddles the fence of what she is saying and what she cannot, will not, must not say.

She had known Fred all of her life. He was a business associate of her father's, a family friend (practically a relative, she observes — the observation draining the light from her eyes as it is enunciated for the first time). Between her fifteenth and sixteenth years the physicality of onrushing womanhood had taken her (and everyone else) by surprise. Fred became a more frequent visitor in their household and his attentions paid to her, while circumspect, became — unmistakably — different. Her anxiety and confusion at this turn of events were compounded by the fact that she seemed to be the only member of the family to note the change.

When she attempted to broach the subject with her father (whose perfection in her eyes was beyond dispute), she found him to be uncharacteristically ill-at-ease with the topic. He deflected her overtures as best he could, mouthing platitudes and non sequiturs with equanimity. When she persisted, became insistent, he cut her off in mid-sentence and advised her that it was a 'woman problem' and told her to 'ask your mother'.

Her mother, while appearing to misdirect the discussion, was actually quite direct (in her circuitous fashion) with her counsel. She cast malicious deprecations and aspersions on all of the boys whose attentions Joanne had inadvertently engaged. She related the woeful history of Great Aunt Agnes' marriage to a ne'er-do-well, a brigand 'silver of tongue and lazy as the day is long'. She asserted the tendency of the future to arrive before one was aware that the present was departing. She acknowledged defects in Fred's physical appearance but insisted that 'you can't tell a book by its cover'.

When Joanne attempted to restore her original inquiry to its intended form, characterizing Fred's attentions as 'unwelcome and improper', her mother had slapped her, calling her 'ungrateful' and 'spoiled'. She informed Joanne that Fred was a gentleman who had been instrumental in assisting them to get established in the city, adding that Fred was probably the closest friend her father had in the world. If Joanne couldn't see her way clear to behaving decently towards a man who had been nothing but decent to her family, then… And at this point her mother had burst into tears.

Over a period of tumultuous weeks, Joanne had pieced the conversation together, had realised what was expected of her. Distraught at her inability to break through the barrier her father had erected between them — and around the subject — she watched him, in vain, for any sign of how he felt about the decision she had made. Even on her wedding day, she couldn't tell if he was happy about her betrothal or…

Of course, while you listen to all this — ostensibly attentive and thoughtful — your mind (and your eyes) are elsewhere. The heat wave — the longest in Palnu's history — exists for you as a series of vivid images and an internalized tempest of passion.

'Oh, that breeze sure feels good, doesn't it?'

She **must** know Cerebus can see her breasts. She **must**. She's wearing it on purpose. She wants Cerebus. She wants Cerebus. She wants Cerebus to touch her. She wants Cerebus to make love to her. Maybe it's just an accident. Aye? Nay? How could she **not** know? She likes it. She likes Cerebus to look at her breasts. She isn't happy with her husband. She's happy with Cerebus. She wants Cerebus to make the first move.

'Goodness, this is your fourth glass of lemonade. You must have a sponge in your stomach.'

Just a little bit further and Cerebus will be able to see her nipple. Just a little bit further. She **must** know that Cerebus can see her breast. She's exposing herself to Cerebus. She wants Cerebus. She wants Cerebus to touch her breast. She wants Cerebus to make love to her. She's just waiting for Cerebus to make the first move. She probably fantasizes about making love to Cerebus the way Cerebus fantasizes about making love to her.

'What was I thinking of, putting a long-sleeve blouse over this? It's boiling today.'

Her nipple. Cerebus is looking at her nipple. She knows Cerebus is looking at her nipple. She wants Cerebus to look at her nipple. She's just wondering why it's taking Cerebus so long to make his move. But what if she **doesn't** want Cerebus? What if she slaps Cerebus and then tells Jaka that Cerebus touched her, that Cerebus tried to kiss her?

215

Over and over the same tortured ground: does she or doesn't she? Will she or won't she? In your imaginings it always happens the same way: you call her over to the side of the house to show her something (but what?) and when she bends down to look, you embrace her and kiss her. And then you pull her down onto the soft, warm grass and caress one of her soft, perfect…

Over and over the same tortured ground: does she or doesn't she? Will she or won't she?

So absorbed are you in your anguished speculations it escapes your notice that the heat wave has, at last, broken. Joanne wears more modest coverings which serve only to inflame your interest further.

They're under there. Cerebus knows what they look like and they're under there.

You think of me from time to time.

We have a deal, right? Jaka is happy with Cerebus no matter what.

The only voice in your head is your own.

The first crisp, cool morning of autumn awakens you to the fact that the window of opportunity is closing swiftly.

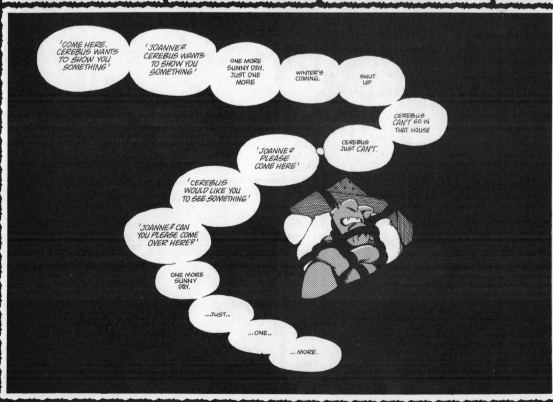

217

218

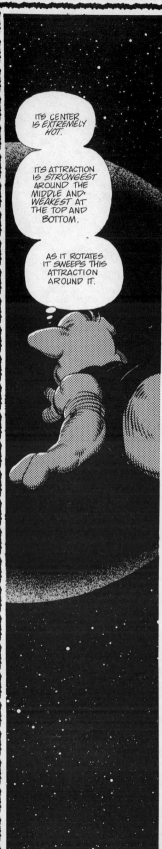

CIRCLING...   ...ENDLESSLY.

WHAT ARE WE GOING TO *DO*?

AH.... YOU *REMEMBER*.

AYE...

YOU SAID, 'WE HAVE TO *KEEP IT A SECRET*'

AND SHE ASKED: (TREMBLING WITH FEAR)

'KEEP *WHAT* A SECRET?'

AND *YOU* ANSWERED...?

'WHAT WE JUST *DID*.'

(THINKING TO YOURSELF 'STUPID LITTLE *SLUT*')

CEREBUS' BACK HURTS.

AND SHE ASKED...?

CEREBUS CAN'T REMEMBER.

SOMETHING STUPID,...

224

...HOURS AGO.

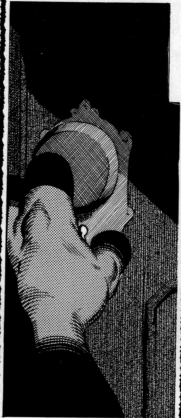

FLMPF

Cerebus

THAT'S JAKA'S HANDWRITING ALL RIGHT.

WELL?

Cerebus

AREN'T YOU GOING TO OPEN IT?

WE HAD A *DEAL.*

'JAKA IS HAPPY TO STAY WITH CEREBUS...'

'...NO MATTER WHAT.'

YES. I KNOW

JUST READ THE LETTER

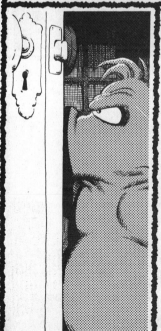

SNIF
SNIF

RIP

RIP
R

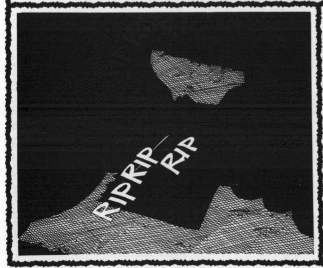

RIPRIP RIP

My Dearest, darling Cerebus —
Whenever I try to tell you how
happy I am to be with you, you

su always get the strangest look in your eyes and change the subject—but it's TRUE! Being with you is the only

thing that makes me happy. I watch you all the time. I know all of your moods by sight. I knew something had changed when you started staring out the window at the house next door. What a pair we would have seemed if anyone had walked in on us! You, there, staring at the house next door and me, here, staring at you. Of course, I never once had to wonder what was on your mind. The look on your face told me all I needed to know—I know

CREAK

WHAT WAS THAT?

JUST KEEP READING ...

that look so well—after all, you used to look at me that way. I finally met Joanne

lly met Joanne

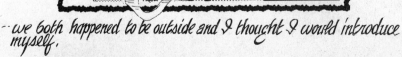

—we both happened to be outside and I thought I would introduce myself.

CREAK

I've never seen such a look of love mingled with fear on a girl's face before,' It's just talking,' she said, 'We just talk!' And then she cringed as if she expected to be hit. I didn't know wh_____say. It really didn't matter to me whe_____ou talked or kissed or Made Love every_____n our bed. Odd, since when I was with Rick (forgive____e, I know you hate for me to mention him)_____erbial Green-Eyed Monster. Your happiness is all that's important to me. I wanted to tell her that.

When she saw I wasn't going to hit her, that look of fear and love turned to one of anger and hate and she said,

'We're not your prisoners you know!'

CREAK

and then I realised, the_____watched you watching her house that my happiness had blinded me to the fact that _your_ happiness now lies elsewhere – with Joanne.
　　I can't leave you.
　　I can't begin to think of a life with someone else or even somewhere else. My only happiness is by your side.
　　I love you, Cerebus, my darling – forever and forever. I never imagined I could be as happy as I've been these last two years

　　　Forgive me,
　　　Jaka

'FORGIVE ME'...

'JAKA'

GIVE...?

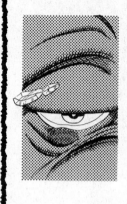

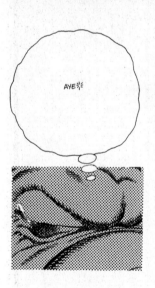

AYE ✱

NO.

YOU *DON'T.*

SEE -- I *KNOW YOU BETTER* THAN THAT.

SIT UP.

PLUTO.

OF THE *SPHERES* OF THE *GODS* IT IS THE MOST *DISTANT* FROM THE SUN. IT IS ALSO THE *SPHERE* WITH THE LEAST MASS.

THE *ODDBALL* SPHERE, THE *HERMIT* SPHERE-- ITS ORBIT *TILTED* SEVENTEEN DEGREES ABOVE THE *ORBITAL PLANE* OF THE OTHER *EIGHT*.

AS IT MOVES *AWAY FROM THE SUN,...*

...ITS *ATMOSPHERE FREEZES* AND FALLS AS *SNOW* ON THE POLAR CAPS.

AT ITS FURTHEST POINT FROM THE SUN IT IS SO COLD THAT THE *ENTIRE* ATMOSPHERE *'FREEZES OUT'*

AND PLUTO IS NOTHING *MORE* THAN A BALL OF *ICE AND ROCK* ADRIFT IN THE *HARD VACUUM* OF SPACE ...

LOOK *BEHIND* YOU.

237

CHARON.

PLUTO'S MOON-- FULLY *HALF* THE SIZE OF PLUTO *ITSELF...*

SO *LARGE* THAT PLUTO AND CHARON ORBIT EACH *OTHER,* SWINGING EACH *OTHER* AROUND A COMMON BALANCE POINT...

SO *CLOSE* THAT THEY SHARE A COMMON ATMOSPHERE (WHEN THAT ATMOSPHERE *EXISTS,* ANYWAY).

TRULY THE *ODDBALL SPHERES* OF THE GODS.

AND YOU *STILL* DON'T UNDERSTAND, *DO YOU? YOU* ARE PLUTO.

IN YOUR IRREGULAR ORBIT, YOU *WARM* SLIGHTLY AND THEN *FREEZE* ONCE MORE INTO THE *AIRLESS, BARREN* EXISTENCE YOU'VE ALWAYS KNOWN.

YOU WANTED *JAKA* TO BE YOUR *CHARON--* TO DERIVE *HER* PLEASURE AND *HER* HAPPINESS FROM SHARING *YOUR* DESOLATION.

I *CHANGED* HER FOR YOU. I *ELIMINATED* HER STATUS AS A PALNAN ARISTOCRAT BECAUSE *YOU* WOULD FIND THAT STATUS *INTOLERABLE.* I *ELIMINATED* HER *DANCING* BECAUSE YOU WOULD FIND HER *DANCING* INTOLERABLE. I *ELIMINATED* YOUR OWN *VIOLENT* NATURE FOR *YOU...*

AND *STILL* IT WASN'T ENOUGH *STILL* IT WOULD *NEVER* BE ENOUGH.

YOUR *INNER* NATURE REMAINED-- YOUR *IGNORANCE,* YOUR *INSENSITIVITY,* YOUR *SELF-ABSORPTION* YOUR...

SHUT UP.

238

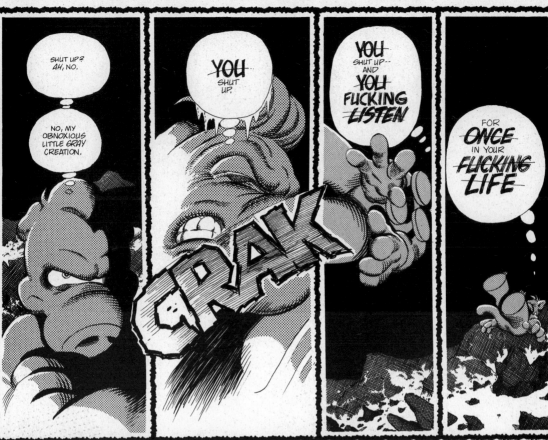

HAVEN'T BEEN HIT *THAT* HARD IN A *LONG* TIME, *HAVE* YOU?

NAY.

WELL, WE'RE RUNNING OUT OF *TIME* -- AND I'M RUNNING OUT OF *WAYS* TO 'WAKE YOU UP'.

SEE, IT'S NOT *ENOUGH* TO SAY, 'I GIVE'...

VERY FRUSTRATING FOR A CREATOR TO *ENGINEER* A CIRCUMSTANCE, THINKING 'AH-- THIS WILL DO THE TRICK... *NOW HE'LL* UNDERSTAND.'

I GO TO ALL THAT TROUBLE ONLY TO *REALISE* THAT YOU HAVEN'T LEARNED A *THING*. YOU 'GIVE' BECAUSE YOU'VE DECIDED *I'M* AGAINST YOU, *TARIM* IS AGAINST YOU -- THE *WORLD* IS AGAINST YOU.

I SCARED YOU, JUST NOW, BY HITTING YOU *VERY* HARD -- AND *THEN* I SCARED YOU SOME *MORE* BY YELLING AT YOU. THE PROBLEM WITH *FEAR* GENERATED BY HITTING AND YELLING IS THAT IT ... WEARS OFF.

OF COURSE (*TEMPORARILY* ANYWAY) YOU ARE IN A STATE OF *HEIGHTENED AWARENESS*... THIS SUDDEN SWITCH, ON *MY* PART, FROM YELLING TO A DISPASSIONATE AND REASONED TONE -- *FAR* FROM *REASSURING* YOU -- IS FEEDING YOUR ANXIETY, AS WELL IT SHOULD.

SO 'AWARE' ARE YOU, THAT A KIND OF *TELEPATHY* EXISTS BETWEEN US. '*CEREBUS* IS *REALLY* IN FOR IT NOW....' INDEED YOU ARE,

'CEREBUS CAN'T GET OUT OF THIS ONE,' INDEED, YOU CAN'T.

'HE KNOWS CEREBUS IS SQUEAMISH ABOUT EYES' INDEED, I DO.

'CEREBUS CAN'T CLOSE HIS RIGHT EYE' INDEED, YOU CAN'T.

240

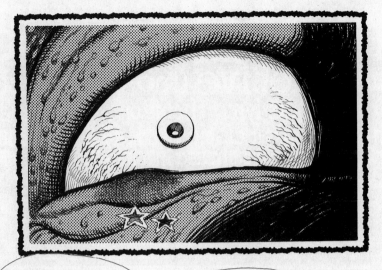

AND *NOW* YOUR STATE OF AWARENESS IS HEIGHTENED EVEN FURTHER, ISN'T IT?

WE HAVE REACHED A POINT OF *THREE-WAY CONVERGENCE.* THERE IS A *BUMP* ON THE UNDERLID OF YOUR RIGHT EYE -- RED AND SWOLLEN AND PAINFUL.

CONSIDER THE *ENTIRETY OF* YOUR PHYSICAL FORM TO BE YOUR CREATOR -- *ME.* CONSIDER THE *BUMP* TO BE YOU...

YOU ARE A PAINFUL RED SWELLING VERY NEAR TO YOUR *CREATOR'S* MOST HIGHLY-DEVELOPED ORGAN OF PERCEPTION...

THE PRESSURE IS BUILDING FROM WITHIN, *GROWING* BY THE MOMENT. *SOMETHING* NEEDS TO BE DONE.

AND *THAT* BRINGS US TO THE *THIRD* PART OF THE CONVERGENCE: 'YOU'.....'ME'

AND A REMARKABLE -- LARGELY FORGOTTEN AND LARGELY *UNFORGETTABLE* -- *QUIRK* IN THE HISTORY OF THE *MEDIUM* WITHIN WHICH YOU EXIST.
TO WIT:

THE 'INJURY-TO-EYE' MOTIF

motif (mō·tēf')

also motive (mō·tĭv', mō·tĕv')

n. 1a) The underlying theme or main element in a literary or artistic work b) A dominant theme 2. A significant phrase in a musical composition 3. A repeated figure or design in architecture or decoration

To describe 'injury to eye' as a 'motif' seems oxymoronic. 'An underlying theme or main element…'? It occurred infrequently in 'crime' and 'horror' comics of the fifties: a panel or two functioning as an archetype of extreme brutality, establishing its perpetrator as an individual devoid of the basics of human empathy. The actual 'theme' of such stories would be described more accurately as 'crime does not pay' or 'bad people come to a bad end'. The supplementary definition — 'a dominant theme' — MIGHT apply if one contemplates the EFFECT of such depictions on the reader/viewer. The shocked, new awareness created by the anticipation of 'injury to eye' imbues the panel or panel sequence with a 'dominance' which exceeds (dramatically) the space it occupies in the story's context. 'A significant phrase in a musical composition': on the surface this seems completely at odds with a soundless medium of expression. But, again, in contemplating the EFFECT upon the reader, the internalized, nearly musical coupling of words and pictures, suddenly conjoined (at an individual level of perception) by a piercing, keening 'gore shriek' (if you will) gives this definition a greater applicability than might be most commonly supposed. How extensive will the injury be? How detailed will the illustration be and at what proximity will it be viewed? The individual reader/viewer's imagination, squeamishness and reluctant anticipation define the boundaries of the 'phrase' and its 'significance'. We will leave discussion of the third definition for the aftermath of this PARTICULAR 'injury to eye'…

scalpel

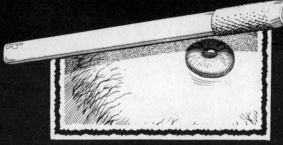

(skal'-pəl) *n.* A small pointed knife with a very sharp thin blade used in dissection and in surgery [L scalpellum dim of scalprum knife < scalpere to CUE]

And now your awareness is heightened even further. Actually, the scalpel comes later in the proceedings. If it's any consolation to you, I went through this myself — twice. The first time, the bump was on my upper lid and (being, like yourself, a slow learner) I didn't get the point (pardon the pun). The second time, there was a bump on my upper **AND** lower lid. With the **LOWER** lid, I got the point.

The point: It is difficult for a creator to engineer a suitable repercussion for the pain which his unfeeling creation has inflicted upon those who feel very deeply and emotionally (please note the accuracy of the term 'repercussion'; the dynamic at work is one of 'cause and effect', not 'punishment').

'Let me show you what you have done unto others,' the creator implies. 'Let me show you all at once.'

So! I have bad news and good news and bad news for you. The **FIRST** bit of bad news is that the scalpel will — very slowly — cut vertically and horizontally through the bump so the blood and pus can be drained from it, the wound irrigated and cleansed.

The **GOOD** news is that you won't feel a thing when it happens. The entire area will be numb — completely insensitive to any pain or sensation whatsoever.

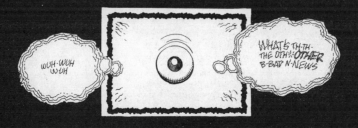

Ah! You see? You're finally paying attention. Isn't heightened awareness grand?

The OTHER bad news (my obnoxious little gray creation) is the

syringe

(sir'inj, si·rinj) *n.*
an instrument (as for the injection of medicine) that consists of a hollow barrel fitted with a plunger and a hollow **needle** [Gk. *syring, syrinx* panpipe, tube]

There are two other supplementary definitions I won't bore you with. The syringe contains an anaesthetic — a solution which will deaden the nerve endings in the afflicted area, completely neutralizing their ability to conduct impulses of pain perception to your brain. The only way to flood the afflicted area with anaesthetic is by means of a hypodermic injection. And the only way to inject it there (and this is OTHER bad news) is through the hollow center of the needle, which must first PIERCE the SOFT FLESH of the underlid.

The second time I went through this, — knowing what was coming — there was a song fragment going through my head before, during and after.

It was the part that goes...

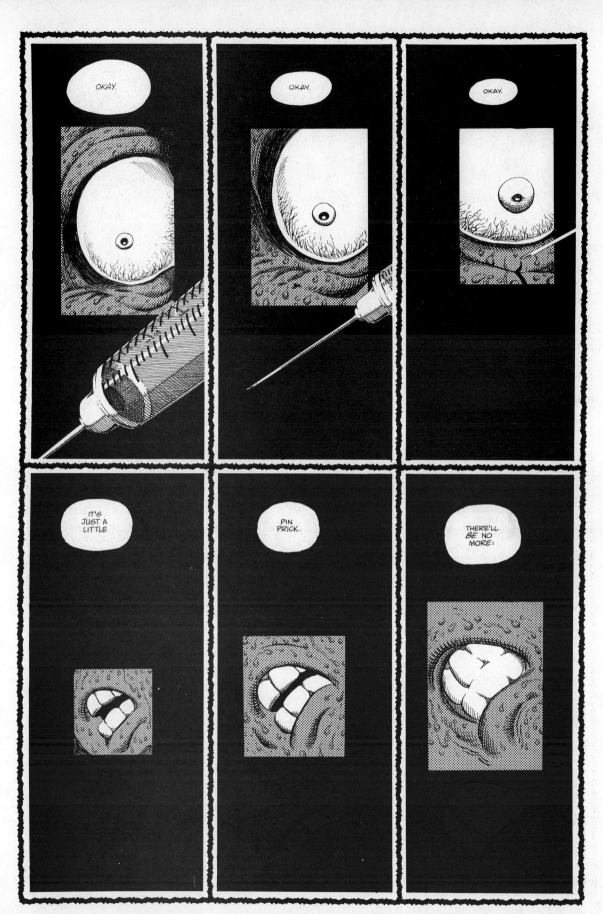

245

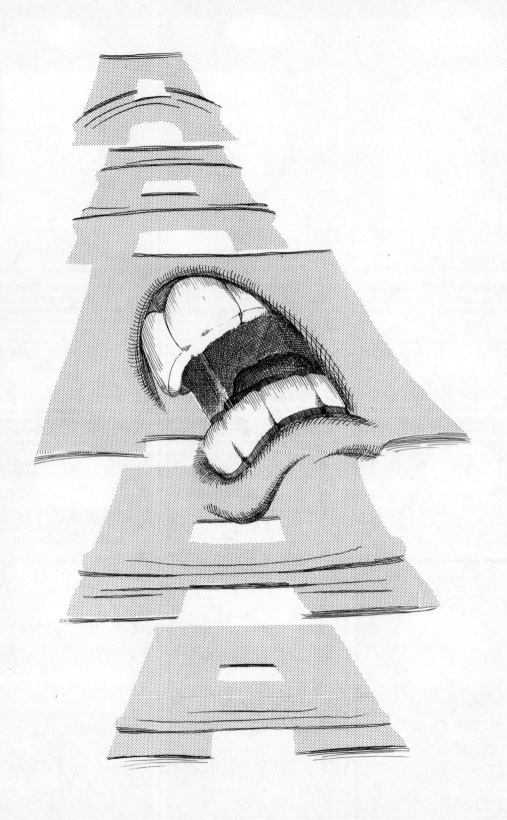

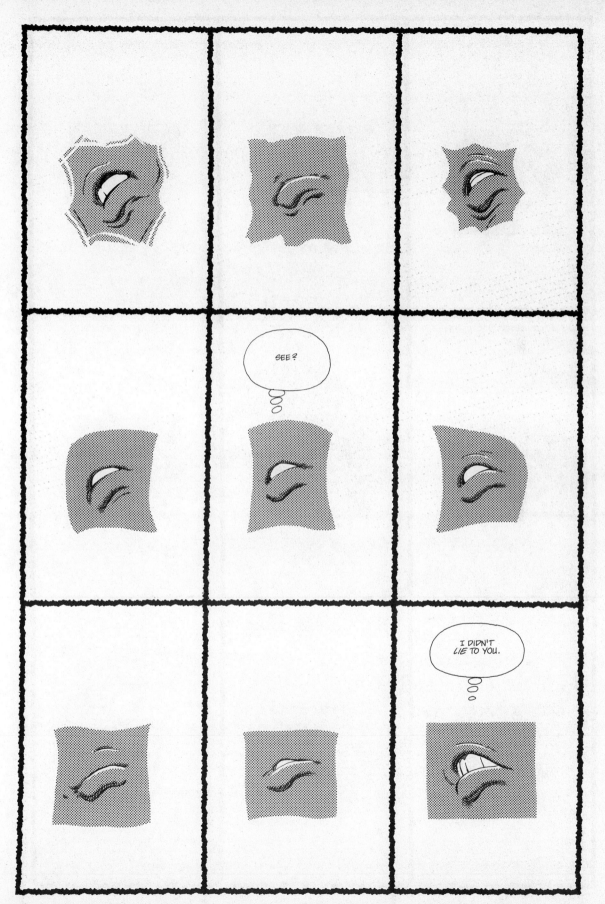

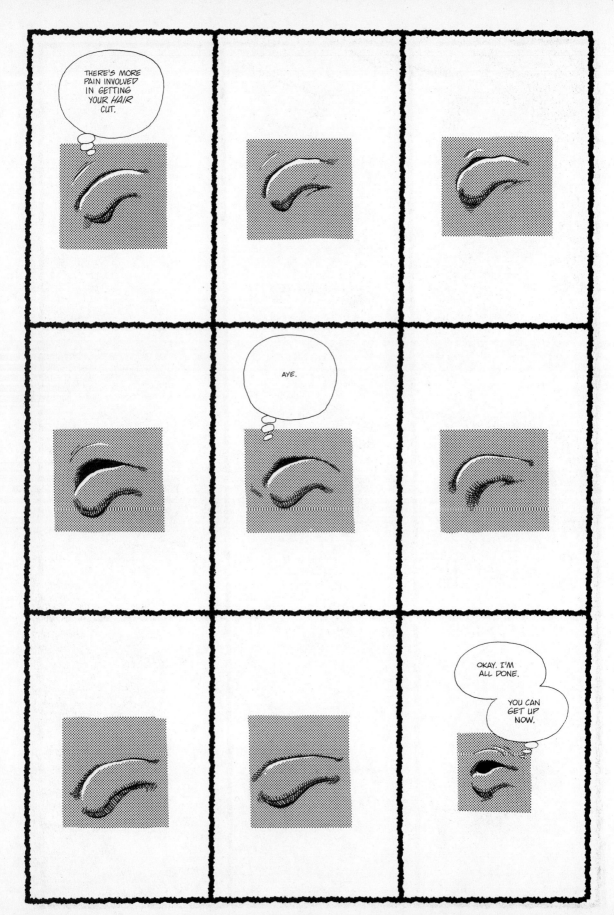

249

'A REPEATED FIGURE IN ARCHITECTURE OR DESIGN'

WITH A *PIN-PRICK*, I SCULPTED A FIGURE IN THE *ARCHITECTURE* OF YOUR MIND, INTRODUCED A *DESIGN* ELEMENT INTO WHAT REMAINS OF YOUR EXISTENCE.

WHETHER IT IS A *REPEATED* FIGURE IS UP TO YOU.

YOU CAN *REMOVE* THE PATCH IN AN HOUR OR SO. THE MINOR DISCOLORATION WILL BE GONE TOMORROW

DOES CEREBUS DIE LIKE THE JUDGE SAID?

YOU MEAN 'ALONE, UNMOURNED AND UNLOVED'?

AYE

WELL, YES, AT THE RATE YOU'RE GOING WHAT *OTHER* ENDING IS POSSIBLE?

WHAT *OTHER* ENDING TO YOUR STORY MAKES SENSE TO *YOU?*

THINK ABOUT IT.

251

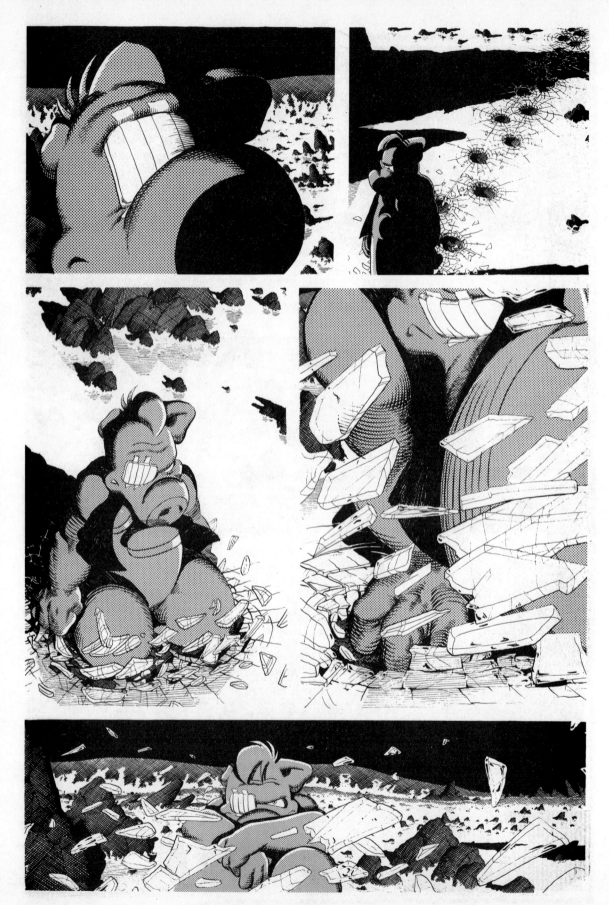

uh-- BASIC *CURIOSITY*-- I ALWAYS WANT TO KNOW WHAT *CHOICE* YOU'RE GOING TO MAKE.... WHAT YOU'RE GOING TO DO *NEXT*.

AS YOU GET *OLDER* IT BECOMES EVEN *MORE* INTERESTING, WILL YOU *IMPROVE* AS YOU GO ALONG? GET *WORSE?* STAY THE SAME?

ARE YOU EVEN *CAPABLE* OF SETTING A DESTINATION FOR YOURSELF? *THAT'S* THE REASON I TOLD YOU THAT YOU HAVE ONLY TO...

uh

GOING SOMEWHERE?

AYE.

MM.

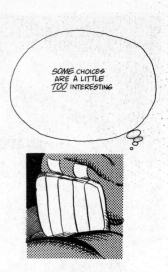

259

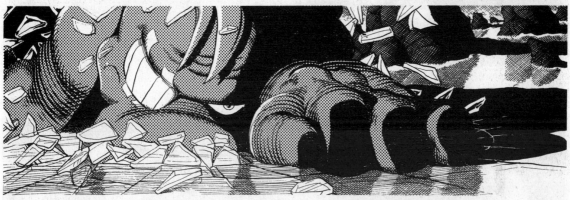

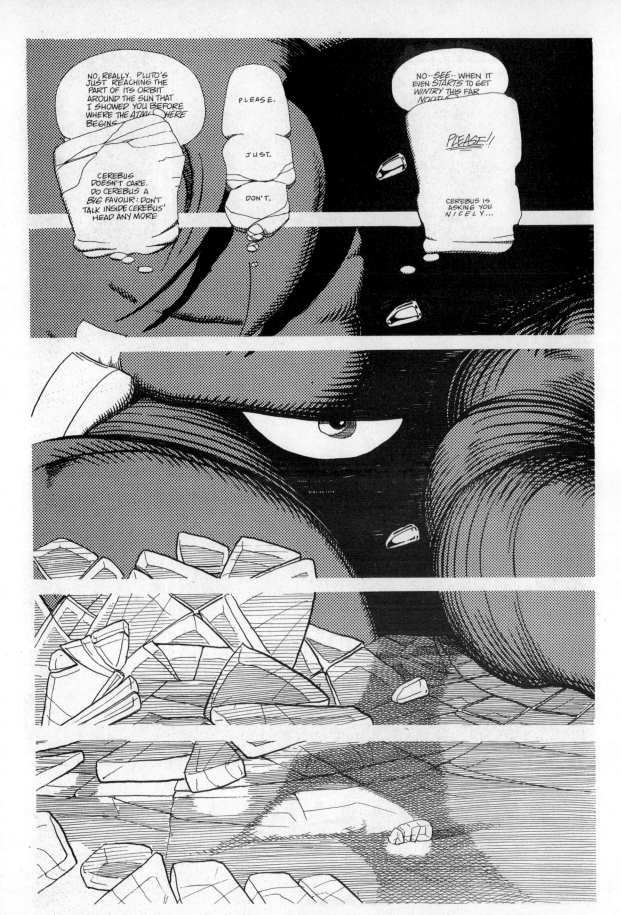

epilogue

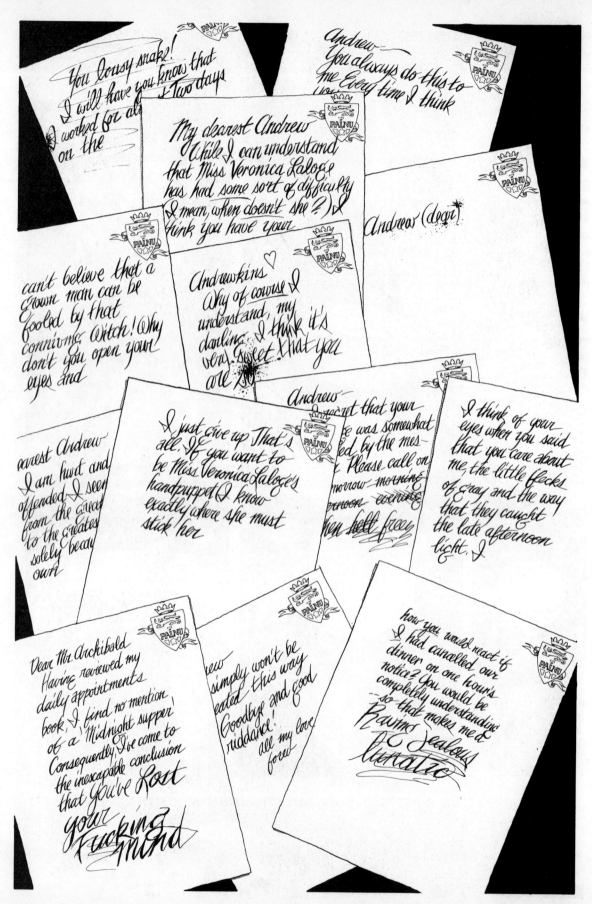

PLUTO.

(THREE WEEKS LATER)

AARDVARK-VANAHEIM.

HELLO IS THIS THE PLACE THAT DOES CEREBUS?

YES IT IS.

THIS IS CEREBUS CALLING. CEREBUS WOULD LIKE TO SPEAK TO DAVE'S BOSS PLEASE.

PLEASE, DAVE

PLEASE SEND CEREBUS BACK TO *ESTARCION.*

TO *ESTARCION.* '''

''' *NOT JAKA.*

CEREBUS *FINALLY* UNDERSTANDS

YOU *DO?*

OH, AYE.

CEREBUS HAS WASTED YEARS--*YEARS*--WAITING FOR SOMEONE WHO DOESN'T *LOVE* HIM -- WHO PROBABLY NEVER *DID* LOVE HIM -- TO COME *BACK*

'ALONE. UNMOURNED. AND UNLOVED.'

THAT'S WHAT THE JUDGE *MEANT* ISN'T IT?

IF CEREBUS KEEPS JUST... *WAITING*... FOR JAKA TO COME *BACK*, CEREBUS IS *ALWAYS* GOING TO BE *ALONE.*

IF CEREBUS NEVER MAKES FRIENDS WITH ANY-ONE, HOW CAN CEREBUS EXPECT TO BE ANYTHING *BUT* 'UNMOURNED'?

IF CEREBUS NEVER *TRIES* TO LOVE ANYONE *BESIDES* JAKA, WHO'S GOING TO LOVE CEREBUS *BACK?*

RIGHT?

AYE-- CEREBUS UNDERSTANDS NOW, DAVE.

CEREBUS IS SORRY HE CALLED YOU 'EVIL', IF YOU HADN'T SHOWED CEREBUS WHAT YOU SHOWED HIM -- CEREBUS WOULD HAVE JUST *WASTED* THE REST OF HIS LIFE *WAITING* FOR JAKA -- CEREBUS SINCERELY APOLOGIZES

IT'S NOT THE *FIRST* TIME I'VE BEEN CALLED 'EVIL' AND I DOUBT IT WILL BE THE *LAST* -- BUT (ANYWAY) --

APOLOGY ACCEPTED.

AYE? GOOD.

I'LL SEND YOU *BACK* WHENEVER YOU LIKE, THE LITTLE TAVERN AT THE *WALL OF TSI* -- JUST BELOW CASTLE WALLIS ?

AYE.

CEREBUS WILL BE A *LOT* BETTER *THIS* TIME, CEREBUS IS NO *SAINT* -- BUT YOU'LL SEE. CEREBUS CAN BE *VERY* NICE WHEN HE *WANTS* TO BE.

THAT'S *VERY* TRUE.

NO MORE GETTING A *LITTLE BIT* WARM AND THEN SNOWING ALL OVER HIMSELF FOR *CEREBUS*...

NO*sir*. CEREBUS IS GOING TO BE WARM *ALL* THE TIME.

SEE THAT LITTLE GRAY GUY OVER THERE (PEOPLE WILL SAY)? HE'S VERY, VERY WARM.

EVERYONE IS GOING TO BE CEREBUS' FRIEND.

EVERYONE.

WHEN CEREBUS WALKS DOWN THE 'ROYAL MILE' TO WALLIS CASTLE, EVERYONE WILL SAY 'HIYA, CEREBUS,' 'HOW'S IT GOING, CEREBUS?'

WELL THAT'S GREAT,... NOW ALL YOU HAVE TO DO IS JUMP OFF OF THE ROCK YOU'RE ...

'LOOK, EVERYONE! IT'S CEREBUS!' 'WE LOVE YOU CEREBUS!' 'HOWDY, CEREBUS!' 'YOU'RE LOOKING MIGHTY FINE TODAY, CEREBUS!'

LISTEN. I HATE TO INTERRUPT YOUR,... PARADE, BUT WE'RE RUNNING OUT OF SPACE HERE.

SORRY.

SORRY.

AGAIN, CEREBUS SINCERELY APOLOGIZES. WHAT WERE YOU SAYING?

YOU JUST HAVE TO JUMP OFF OF THE ROCK YOU'RE STANDING ON --

YOU'LL DRIFT DOWN THROUGH THE 'WHITENESS' FOR A WHILE AND THE NEXT THING YOU KNOW YOU'LL BE RIGHT OUTSIDE THE TAVERN ...

REALLY?

UH-HUH.

THANKS, DAVE. CEREBUS REALLY MEANS IT. THANKS-- FOR THE NEEDLE IN CEREBUS' EYE, JAKA'S NEW BOYFRIEND, ABANDONING CEREBUS ON JUNO -- THANK YOU, DAVE FOR EVERYTHING.

SO JUMP ALREADY.

RIGHT YOU ARE.